Great Quarterbacks #2
KILMER   BRADSHAW
TARKENTON   LAMONICA

Bill Gutman

tempo
books

GROSSET & DUNLAP
A National General Company
Publishers   New York

To Frank Yohan,
a number one football fan
and number one guy

Acknowledgments

The author wishes to thank the following people for their help in supplying background material for this book: Joe Browne and Kay O'Reilly of the National Football League office; the publicity departments of the Washington Redskins, Minnesota Vikings, Pittsburgh Steelers, and Oakland Raiders; Keith Prince, Sports Information Director at Louisiana Polytechnic Institute; Dan Magill, Sports Information Director at the University of Georgia; and the sports information departments at Notre Dame University and UCLA.

CONTENTS

1 Billy Kilmer 1

2 Terry Bradshaw 47

3 Fran Tarkenton 91

4 Daryle Lamonica 139

5 Statistics 183

BILLY KILMER

Bill Kilmer has always had a reputation as a certain kind of guy. His guts and determination have been admired and respected for a long time, even before he attained his current star status with the Washington Redskins.

One of the greatest of all professional quarterbacks, Bart Starr, used to tell a story on the banquet circuit whenever someone asked him how he became the Packer quarterback. The tale really had no connection with Kilmer, that is, until a former pro football coach heard it one night. It went something like this:

"When Coach Lombardi came to Green Bay the first thing he did was build a large brick wall at the end of the field. Then he told all the players to run toward it full tilt. The ones who banged into it and fell backwards became defensive lineman. Those who cracked into it and fell on their stomachs became offensive linemen. The ones who ran through it were the fullbacks, and the ones who ran up to the wall, stopped, then walked around it became quarterbacks."

After hearing this story one night, the former coach grinned and remarked, "Lombardi would have been thoroughly confused if he sent Billy Kilmer at that wall. Billy would run into it, run through it, jump over it, or walk around it . . . anything that it took to win. Lombardi wouldn't have known where to play him."

Vince Lombardi never coached Billy Kilmer. If he had, however, he would have known exactly where to play him. For one way or another, Billy Kilmer is a quarterback. He may defy convention; he may not have the natural physical attributes; he may do things his own way—but Kilmer is all quarterback.

Washington Redskin tight end, Jerry Smith, no little guy himself, once looked at a bruised and battered Kilmer coming into the locker room after a game and said, "If it was three o'clock in the morning and I had to go down a dark alley, I'd want him with me."

That kind of respect doesn't come easy, but William Orland Kilmer earned it, and he didn't do it the easy way. After all, it's not many quarterbacks who are told:

They may not live.

They may lose a leg.

They will never play football again.

And it isn't every quarterback who can sit on a professional bench for the better part of three seasons seeing less action than the water boy, then bounce back with a display of skills people never knew existed. But Billy Kilmer did it.

On December 24, 1972, an overflow crowd gathered in Washington's Robert F. Kennedy Stadium to watch their beloved Redskins do battle with the Green Bay Packers in the first round of the National Conference playoffs.

The hometown fans hooted and cheered as each Redskin starter was introduced and trotted onto the field. But they saved the longest and loudest cheers for number 17, their quarterback, a 33-year-old veteran named Billy Kilmer.

Fans watching Kilmer jog confidently onto the field and begin exhorting his teammates with shouts and smacks on the back wouldn't have known it was the same man who, exactly 10 years earlier, lay flat on his back in a San Francisco hospital fighting for his life, his leg, and his professional career. Lombardi's brick wall would have looked awfully big to him then.

Kilmer had come to the Skins in 1971, in the first of many trades engineered by new head coach George Allen. After struggling at San Francisco and taking his lumps with expansionist New Orleans, Kilmer should have been happy going to the rebuilding Redskins. But he wasn't, and that was because the Washington team had a quarterback named Sonny Jurgensen, widely regarded as one of the best passers ever. The thought of once again being a backup didn't appeal to this competitive fireball from Topeka, Kansas.

But Allen knew what he wanted. When someone questioned the trade, the coach snapped, "Kilmer is a fighter. He never quits. He's done a tremendous job at New Orleans. He's the kind of competitor and leader I want around here. No matter where I was coaching I'd want him. He'll be ready whenever we need him."

The need came. An injury to Jurgensen in the exhibition season made Kilmer number one for the entire 1971 season. And what did he do? He led the Washington Redskins to their best record in 29 years and into the NFL playoffs. Like the man said, when they needed him, Billy Kilmer was ready.

There was a time when William Orland Kilmer wasn't ready. It was by no fault of his, however. Bad luck seemed to dog the gritty quarterback from the beginning of his career.

Not from the beginning of his life, though. That was a happy time. Billy was born in Topeka on September 5, 1939. When he was just a youngster his parents moved to California where his father, Orland Kilmer, opened a dry cleaning business. Mr. Kilmer was away from home some 10 to 12 hours a day, and when young Bill saw his first football game it was with his grandfather at the Los Angeles Coliseum.

"I guess I was about five then," Bill recalls. "I know that my feet wouldn't even reach the floor when I sat in the chair. Anyway, my grandfather took me to the game and I can remember sitting in the crowded stands and thinking even then that I wanted to be just like those football players on the field. It just looked so great to be playing in front of so many people. I told my grandfather that I wanted to be a football player when I grew up. I don't know if he believed me, but we were always great pals and he took me to a game almost every week."

Grandpa Kilmer wasn't the only member of the family to encourage young Bill in athletics. His mother had once pitched on a ladies softball team that won the Women's World Series at Soldier Field in Chicago, and she still got a kick out of pitching the ball to her son in the backyard of their home. So that took care of football and baseball.

Orland Kilmer handled the basketball end of it. He put up a board and hoop in the yard and Billy used to shoot at it for hours on end.

"It was a great way to relieve my frustrations," said Billy. "Whenever I wanted to think about something or make some plans, I'd go out and shoot baskets. That's when I got my ideas."

And that wasn't all. Mr. Kilmer had been Missouri Valley Swimming champion and once had an opportunity to try out for the Olympic team. As a result, swimming came easily to Bill and he could hold his own in the water with anyone.

When he got to junior high school he began putting his all-around athletic skills to work and he quickly found out something about himself.

"I loved competition," Bill recalls, "right from the first. It was the challenge to win. I always wanted to be the very best at everything I did."

When Billy arrived at Azusa High School, he was a multi-sport star, a performer for all seasons who electrified the Azusa fans with his exploits on the playing fields. At first, the six-foot, 190-pound Kilmer preferred basketball. He liked the constant movement and hectic non-stop action of the court game. He was a standout at guard, ball-handling, driving, and jump-shooting with the best of them. He led the Azusa team to a near-perfect record for three seasons. The team lost just one league game in that time and Kilmer became Southern California scoring champion, pumping nearly 2,000 points through the hoop in three seasons.

But he didn't neglect the other sports. He may not have liked baseball as much, but he played the game with consummate skill. In fact, by the time he was a senior the scouts were coming around in droves and the word on Kilmer was out. There was talk of a $50,000 bonus with the Pirates, and Billy liked the sound of that.

"I was all set to sign and leave for training camp," he revealed, "but my mother intervened. She was determined that I go to college and my father agreed. Then I thought it out and decided it was the right thing.

"Besides, by then I was really in love with football.

That's why I chose UCLA. They still played the single wing formation and I wanted a chance to be a tailback. I wanted to be a triple-threat man—running, passing, and kicking. There weren't too many if those guys left anymore."

So, after a year at Citrus Junior College, Billy went to UCLA with the prime objective of playing tailback. But what is a tailback? You don't really hear the term much anymore.

That's because the single wing as an offensive formation is almost completely gone today. All schools use the standard "T," the pro set, the wishbone-T, or some other variation. But in each of these cases, the play is started by the quarterback taking a direct snap from the center.

With the single wing, the quarterback was merely a blocking back, standing to the right or left of center and calling signals. He rarely touched the ball on offense. The focal point of the attack was the tailback, who stood about five yards behind the center and took a direct snap. From there, the tailback would either run, throw, or kick when necessary. Occasionally, he'd hand the ball to his fullback, who stood in the backfield with him. But more than 90 percent of the time, the tailback started the play.

When Kilmer arrived at UCLA, there were still a handful of college teams using the single wing. The UClans were among them, and there Bill could realize his long-standing dream of playing tailback. Coach George Dickerson knew the multi-talented halfback from Azusa could do it all, and immediately installed him as a tailback candidate during his sophomore year of 1958.

By the end of the practice season, Bill had won the starting tailback job and opened the season against the

University of Pittsburgh. It looked as if his dream was about to come true. On the first series of downs, Bill began marching the Bruins downfield. With the ball on the 40, he took a direct snap, dropped back another two or three yards, then heaved a long pass to his flanker back. The receiver gathered it in at the goal line and went over for a score.

Billy came to the sidelines, the cheers of the crowd ringing like music in his ears. He was proud and happy, and thought back to the days when his grandfather used to take him to the games. His grandfather and the rest of his family were in the stands that day and it made Billy even happier.

The UClans eventually lost that one, 27-6, but Kilmer had shown enough to win the regular tailback job. The rest of the team was young and inexperienced, but Billy was happy to be in there. He had a fine second game, helping defeat Illinois, 18-14, and with a win under his belt, looked forward to meeting another single win team, Oregon State, the next week.

Then, early in the game it happened. There was a pileup on a running play and Bill got up holding his right hand. Someone had stepped on it and he left the game. X-rays showed a broken bone and he was out. Terribly disappointed, the combative Kilmer had to sit the bench until the final game. Against USC he saw limited action, played well, and was instrumental in helping his team to a 15-15 deadlock.

Bill was happy to be back, but he was also thinking of the next season and a chance to redeem himself for what he considered a lost year. There were those who agreed with him; a local paper said, "Nothing is going to stop Billy Kilmer next year."

With a new coach in Bill Barnes and a more experienced team, the Bruins looked to a big year. Barnes was counting on Kilmer as his starting tailback. Then fate took a hand once again.

Umpiring an intramural baseball game, Bill was struck on his ankle by a foul ball. The ankle wasn't broken, but bruised severely enough to shelve him once again. This time he couldn't run, and by the time the season was almost over, he was out of shape and overweight. He struggled to get ready, and with the ankle still tender, managed to get into the last five games.

He saw some action against Stanford and North Carolina State, then came back against unbeaten USC. Playing in sneakers because his ankle was too sore for football cleats, the gutty Kilmer hobbled through a few running plays. But mostly he passed—and he was on target. When the day ended, the Bruins were 10-3 winners, and Kilmer shared the glory with the UCLA defense, which had bottled up the Trojan attack most of the afternoon.

Bill did the same thing the following two weeks, helping to defeat Utah, 21-6, then participating in a losing effort against Syracuse, 36-8. But the club had improved and managed a 5-4-1 record with everyone looking forward to the 1960 season. One writer, however, voiced cautious optimism, something everyone felt.

"For two seasons now," he wrote, "the Bruins have had a potentially outstanding tailback in young Bill Kilmer. When he's right, the experts say he's at least the equal of Paul Cameron, Primo Villanueva, Sam Brown, and Ronnie Knox, the top tailbacks since the Bruins began using the single wing a dozen years ago.

"But Kilmer has never had a chance to really show his stuff. The injury jinx has hit this youngster from Azusa, and hit him hard. A broken hand and severely bruised ankle have cost him the better part of two seasons. Now, as a senior, he has one last chance to show that he rates with the best. Let's hope he stays healthy ... for everyone's sake."

He stayed healthy. It took a few games for him to get the feel of being a fulltime tailback, and the defense had to mature, too, but the Bruins soon showed signs of being one of the best teams in the country, with Kilmer the spirtual and physical leader.

UCLA opened with an 8-7 win over Pittsburgh, then tied Purdue at 27-all. A 10-8 loss to Washington followed, so the team was 1-1-1 after three games. But Kilmer was already making his mark. He fired three TD passes in the deadlock with Purdue, and according to most observers, outplayed Washington QB Bob Schloredt even though the Bruins lost.

After a 26-8 victory over Stanford, the Bruins edged North Carolina State, 7-0, as Billy outplayed State's Roman Gabriel, considered by many as the best T-quarterback in the country. Two big victories followed that, a 28-0 win over California, and a 22-0 whitewash of the Air Force Academy. And suddenly Kilmer was attracting national attention.

Though statistics are not really a true measure of a player's worth, in Bill's case they helped. Because his combined running and passing yardage put him near the top of the pack in the race for national total offense leader. A healthy Kilmer was proving the experts right. He was one of the best.

A loss to arch-rival USC followed, but Kilmer and the Bruins then closed out the year with wins over Utah and Duke. The team was 7-2-1 for the season and Kilmer had taken the total offense title.

Playing in all 10 Bruin games, Billy had carried the ball 163 times for 803 yards, averaging nearly five yards a carry. In addition, he completed 64 of 129 passes for 1,086 yards and eight touchdowns. His total was 1,889 yards, and he took the total offense crown by more than 150 yards. He completed his dream of being a triple-threat star by punting for a 42.3 yard average on 35 kicks, and that was good for fifth best in the entire country.

And he got more recognition than that. Coach Barnes called him the best tailback UCLA ever had. He was named to the Football Writers' Association and *Sporting News* All-America teams. On four occasions he was Southern California Player of the Week, and five times he was named Big Five Back of the Week. But it wasn't only on the coast. He was a two-time Associated Press National Back of the Week and twice a member of the UPI Backfield of the Week. It was quite a year, and the end of an era as well. Kilmer was the last great single wing tailback at UCLA. Soon after he left the UClans switched to the straight-T formation, as most colleges were changing their style of play.

What to do now? After all, the pros didn't play the single wing. It was the straight-T all the way in the NFL. There was a time when Bill planned to go into the dry cleaning business with his father, but now football was in his blood. He had to give it a try. He was married by then, and had an infant daughter. He worried about his wife and child, but since he had the family business to fall back upon, nothing would be lost if football didn't work out.

The main problem was finding a position. He knew he could run the ball and he knew he could throw. But could he do either well enough to play halfback or quarterback in the pros? Many of the scouting reports read: Too slow to be a halfback; not a strong enough arm to be a quarterback. It looked like a dead end.

There were other T-quarterbacks that year, men like

Fran Tarkenton and Norman Snead, and they were grabbed right away by the pros. Kilmer figured he'd have to wait. But then he heard the news. The San Francisco 49ers, a better-than-average club, picked him as their first draft choice.

Billy couldn't believe it. He knew that the 49ers had two fine quarterbacks in veteran Y. A. Tittle and young John Brodie. They also seemed set at halfback. He wondered just what they had planned for him.

It didn't take him long to find out. San Francisco coach Red Hickey called on Billy and explained what he had in mind. Hickey thought football was ready for a change. He planned to open the 1961 season with a new offensive formation. It was tabbed the "Shotgun," and would feature the quarterback taking a direct snap from center.

"You mean it's similar to the single wing?" an astonished Billy asked.

"Similar," said Hickey, "in that I'll need a quarterback who can run as well as pass."

"I'm your man," said Billy. And suddenly he had a new lease on life.

The shotgun wasn't a new formation. It was similar to the old double-wing, giving the offensive team an extra wide receiver. The immortal Glenn "Pop" Warner had used it at Stanford right after World War I, and several other colleges had used it on occasion. It was known as a potent passing formation, the theory being that the passer didn't have to turn his back on the field as the T-quarterback often does while retreating. The shotgun passer could watch his receivers throughout the entire pattern.

Of course, he didn't have as many options on running plays. That's why the shotgun triggerman (you couldn't really call him a quarterback) had to be able to lug leather himself. Put those prerequisites into the 1960 collegiate hopper and the answer came out K-I-L-M-E-R.

The situation with the 49ers was strangely parallel to something that had happened some 20 years earlier. The year was 1940 and Stanford University was using the double-wing formation. There was a 175-pound kid named Frankie Albert on the squad. Since he was so small they didn't know what to do with him. Then new coach Clark Shaughnessy decided to switch to the T. In Albert, he found a perfect quarterback.

Frankie went on to the 49ers and a great career as a lefthanded passer in the National Football League. The T had saved Albert's career, and now it looked as if the shotgun might save Kilmer's.

Billy was excited about beginning his professional career. But he had a stop to make first. Because of his all-around ability he was chosen to play in the annual College All-Star Game in Chicago, with the top collegians going against the world champion Philadelphia Eagles. At practice, Kilmer so impressed Coach Otto Graham that he installed Billy behind Norman Snead at the quarterback position, the T-quarterback position.

Philadelphia quickly took a lead, pushing around the inexperienced collegians without much trouble. It soon became evident that Snead couldn't move the All-Stars. Graham knew he had to shake up his team so he replaced the classic passer with the street fighter. Billy Kilmer went into the game.

Suddenly the stars seemed to come to life. With Kilmer handing the ball off, carrying it himself, and throwing, they began to move. Three times they drove upfield. The first two times the Eagle defense stiffened and held. The third time they couldn't stop Kilmer. He passed for first downs on three consecutive plays as the huge crowd roared. The Stars jumped to the line breathing fire. Kilmer barked signals, took the snap, and ran straight up the middle through the heart of the Philly defense, picking up 13 yards and another first down.

Like most great players, Kilmer is an opportunist. He knew the Eagles were down and he wanted to strike fast. He took the snap and dropped straight back. Playing the unfamiliar T didn't seem to bother him at all. He looked downfield and rifled a pass to Glynn Gregory in the end zone. Touchdown! Kilmer had thrown for a 17-yard score and the Stars were on the board.

His leadership continued throughout the rest of the game, and he drove his team to another late score. The final was 28-14 in favor of the Eagles, but Kilmer was the talk of the town. He was voted the Most Valuable All-Star Performer, something very few people would have bet on before the game began. But Billy was never one to rest on his laurels. After the game he headed right for the 49er camp, ready to start all over again.

When he got there he found that Coach Hickey was indeed working hard at the new shotgun formation. He had already made one move, deciding that the veteran Tittle was too old and slow to trigger the shotgun, so he traded the old quarterback to the New York Giants. The other triggermen were Brodie, essentially a passer, and a rookie named Bobby Waters, whose forte was running the ball. Kilmer, it seemed, offered the best pass-run combination of the three.

Very few quarterbacks in the NFL can step in and do a job from day one. It takes several years for the T quarterback to learn all the intricacies of his trade. Some never learn. But when Billy lined up in the shotgun for the first time he felt right at home. The players were bigger, faster, and stronger, but otherwise he could have sworn it was UCLA all over again.

"Since I was a single-wing tailback in college," Bill said, "this is the only possible formation that I could step into without a long period of training."

Before long, the roles of the three rotating quarterbacks became obvious. Brodie was a professional thrower all right, by far the best pure passer in the group. But he wasn't a runner of any sort. He could scamper for shelter when pursued, but couldn't do much on designed running plays. Waters, on the other hand, was quite a fine runner who might have had a shot at a halfback job. But his passing left something to be desired and it was a risk any time he threw the football.

Kilmer easily presented the best combination as triggerman. He wasn't a speed merchant and didn't have the fine moves of a Hugh McElhenny, but he knew how to run and he had guts. He'd gain yardage. And his passing was certainly above average. They said he didn't have the arm to be a pro quarterback, but he had shown more than adequate poise and passing in the All-Star game, and he was doing it again from the shotgun.

Brodie could pass; Waters could run—but it was Kilmer who moved the team.

San Francisco opened the season with a flourish as the shotgun put points on the scoreboard in bunches. And early in the season it became obvious that Kilmer was more or less the regular. Brodie came in on some passing situations, Waters when a fresh runner was needed. Kilmer himself ran much more often than he passed, but the threat of the pass was present on every play and that made him more effective.

The team was in the running during the early part of the year, but after the halfway point, some of the other clubs began to catch up with the shotgun. Most observers figured the newness of the formation accounted for its effectiveness in the early going.

"What did you expect," wrote one newsman. "Most teams work at defensing the T. That's what they see, week after week. Suddenly, along comes the shotgun and takes them by surprise. But give them a few weeks to study it, learn what makes it tick, and they'll be ready, even the teams that haven't seen it before. That's what makes these guys pros."

But while there was now some doubt about the ultimate success of the formation, there was no doubt about Bill Kilmer's ability to run it. Just past the midseason mark, league statistics showed that Billy was number six in the league rushing race.

"Pro football hasn't been easy for me," said the flashy rookie. "I've learned more here already than I did in my entire career before this. But with Coach Hickey calling the plays, I can concentrate strictly on execution and I think that's helped."

Someone asked Billy if he didn't think the shotgun was too predictable since he ran so much more than he passed.

"I'm not sure about that. We'll have to see. But I'll tell you one thing. I threw the ball more often than a T quarterback runs. So the defense has to be ready for both."

The last few weeks of the season were tough ones. The offense wasn't moving nearly as well as it had earlier and many were beginning to think the shotgun had run its course. The team finished with a mediocre 7-6-1 record, winding up fifth in the Western Conference of

the NFL. What had been a season of great expectations
turned into a disappointment.

Though one scribe called Bill "the first quarterback
since Sammy Baugh to attain instant stardom," there
were some low points. First of all, the team didn't win.
And winning always meant everything to Billy. And
secondly, he wondered if he could accurately be called
a quarterback. With the future of the shotgun in doubt,
he could easily become a player without a position.

Statistically, he had an outstanding year. He had carried the ball 96 times, gaining 509 yards on an average
of 5.3 yards per carry. And he was the bread-and-but-
ter man around the goal line, scoring 10 touchdowns,
including a record four in one game against the Vikings.

In the passing department, he really didn't have the
chance to prove much, throwing just 34 times and completing 19 for 286 yards. Some quarterbacks do as
much in a single game.

Tight end Mike Ditka of the Chicago Bears was the
Rookie of the Year that season, and Bill couldn't even
claim to be the best rookie quarterback. Fran Tarkenton, the freshman signal-caller of the Vikings, passed
for almost 2,000 yards, and 18 touchdowns, and
scrambled for 308 on the ground. When they met head
to head, Kilmer helped San Francisco produce two victories, 38-24, and 38-28.

Yet Billy must have wondered what the future held.
He was somewhat in limbo and wanted a chance to
prove himself again. He'd have to, especially if the
shotgun was abandoned.

It wasn't. Hickey wanted to give it one more try in
1962, and Billy again figured large in his plans. The
young tailgunner went into the new year full of optimism, but before long he realized that it was just

more of the same. In fact, it was worse. The team wasn't putting nearly as many points on the board, and it was giving up more. They weren't winning, and it was becoming obvious that the shotgun was slowly grinding to a halt.

Billy was the same kind of player in 1962. He ran much more often than he passed, and ran effectively. On the rare occasions that he did throw, his passes were wobbly, but accurate.

By the time the club had completed its first 12 games, Bill's stats were comparable to those of his rookie season. He had rushed 93 times for 478 yards and a 5.1 average, scoring five touchdowns along the way. Passing, he was just eight of 13 for 191 yards, but that was good for another score. Although there were still two games left, it was apparent that the 49ers were not going to play .500 ball. (They finished at 6-8.)

Billy Kilmer didn't play in those final two games. In fact, for a long while it looked as if he had played his last football game ever. Bill didn't know it when he finished practice the afternoon of December 5, 1962, but he was about to embark on the biggest battle of his young life.

He left camp and began driving to the city on the Bayshore Freeway. Bill was a tired man. The team had a couple of days off before the practice and he had been on a quick hunting trip. He was drowsy as he whipped the auto along the freeway at a fast clip. It's not clear just what happened next. A car might have veered into his path, or he might have fallen asleep, but in a flash, Kilmer's car was off the road and careening down a steep embankment.

The car rolled some 435 feet through a field and into a deep ditch. In the car lay an unconscious Bill Kilmer, with a right leg badly fractured above the ankle, a severely slashed chin, and a deep gash over his right eye. He was also suffering from concussion and shock.

When rescue workers arrived, they had to use a crowbar and torch to get Kilmer out of the car. In that time muddy water from the ditch had seeped into the auto and was already causing infection in the leg. It was a nightmare.

"I'm sure I fell asleep at the wheel," Billy recalled later. "The car went off the road and began plunging into the ditch. I remember waking up as I went off. I knew if I let go of the wheel I'd be thrown out, so I held on. I figured if I went flying out anything could happen. Anyway, my right leg got caught under the brake pedal. I could feel it snap, and I could see the bone coming through."

When the doctors first examined him they weren't sure whether they could save the leg. They set the bones, and there was no real ligament damage. But the muddy water had started an infection. If it couldn't be controlled, the situation would be crucial.

Billy lay in the hospital bed for the next few days thinking about just one thing. Then he started asking questions. First he asked about the leg. They told him they could save it unless there were more complications. Then he asked about walking. They told him he'd probably never walk normally again. Finally, he asked the big one. He wanted to know if he'd ever play football again. The doctors said there was no chance.

"We'll see about that," Billy Kilmer said to himself.

The hospital stay extended to three months as the leg slowly healed and the danger of more infection ebbed. Billy just lay there all those days and not a minute passed in which he didn't think about football, about how much he wanted to play again.

"My dad came in one day and asked me what I

planned to do with myself now," he recalls. "I knew, but I didn't tell him. He suggested I come into the dry cleaning business since I always said I would someday. I agreed to work with him, but I was already making plans to rehabilitate the leg."

Billy began hobbling around his father's store. Within three weeks he was doubly convinced that he had to play ball again. But he faced another operation on the leg the following June, this one to remove some floating bone chips that had accumulated. Then the doctor's work would be done. The rest was up to Bill.

He knew there was no chance to play in 1963, and he wasn't even listed on the 49er roster. The team slipped all the way to the bottom of the loop that year as Red Hickey and the shotgun offense were both booted out the door. But Bill couldn't think about that now. His first job was to get himself back into playing shape. He'd worry about a position later.

"I had to look at it that way," he explained. "My life was athletics and I figured I was too young to give it all up. I tend to get a little stubborn, especially about things I really want . . . and this was something I really wanted. Nobody ever came out and said I *couldn't* play football any more. They just said they didn't think I would. Well, I had to find out for myself whether I could or I couldn't."

Bill worked out during 1963 and the early part of '64, pushing himself continually and slowly, ever so slowly, regaining his mobility in the ankle. He knew he might not have as much speed as he once had, but he was prepared to use whatever was left.

Then in July of 1964 it became official. Billy was rejoining the squad and would be a full playing member when training camp opened the following week. The 49ers had a new coach by then, Jack Christiansen, who promptly returned the team to the more traditional T formation. John Brodie would be the quarterback, and a strong-armed youngster from Miami, George Mira, was slated to be the backup. That left Kilmer somewhere between third string and a halfback job.

San Francisco president Lou Spadia talked about Kilmer at a news conference. "The doctors say Billy is sound of limb," said Spadia. "If enthusiasm, courage, and guts can bring him all the way back, then I know he'll make it. In fact, he may be around for a long time."

As soon as camp opened, Christiansen made it known that Billy would be used as a running back only. Kilmer didn't complain. Making the team was his first goal.

In early August the team had its first all-out scrimmage at Kezar Stadium. When Billy entered the game, the fans who had come out to watch gave him a rousing reception. Buoyed by their cheers, the former shotgun triggerman ran well and apparently without pain in his ankle. It was hard to believe. When the scrimmage ended he was the leading runner on the day with 37 yards on seven carries. And on one play he took a handoff, faked an end sweep, and suddenly whipped a 13-yard TD pass to Monty Stickles. Kilmer could still hurt an opponent in more ways than one.

But the music just wasn't there. It was a matter of timing, a new position, and some faster, stronger backs ahead of him. Christiansen used him sparingly all season, though there were those who felt his leadership ability and inspirational play could have helped the team, especially since a 4-10 season kept the 49ers mired in the basement.

As it was, Billy carried just 36 times for 113 yards. As an option passer he was eight of 14 for 92 yards and a score. But it wasn't much of a season. And to add even more confusion to the situation, Christiansen approached him when it was all over and said he wanted him back as a quarterback in '65.

Billy jumped at the news. In his heart, this was what he wanted to do. But he realized it wouldn't be easy. Christiansen treated him like any other player and Bill knew he had to make the team on his own. He survived the final cut, but saw little action in the exhibition games. In the final pre-season game against the Rams he got in long enough to throw three passes. They were the last three he'd throw all year. Brodie and Mira were still ahead of him, and, to make matters even worse, he reinjured the bad ankle. He didn't get in for one play.

By now, even a positive thinker like Bill was becoming discouraged. Going into the 1966 season he was 27 years old and felt that his career hadn't even begun. The years of shotgun seemed like a dream. Now he was a third-string quarterback and it seemed as if he'd always been one. But he wouldn't quit, and when 1966 rolled around he was right back in there plugging.

Before the season started, Coach Christiansen talked about Billy's drawbacks and attributes.

"Bill's been throwing better than ever before this year," the coach said. "He doesn't have the great speed, the quickness, or the straight overarm delivery, but he compensates for all that with a great feel for the game. He's as knowledgeable as they come and has the instinct of good quarterbacks who know when to let go of the ball.

"As a runner he has the same type of feeling and can get away and through holes that others can't. Billy loves the game and is in it from start to finish, even when he's sitting on the bench. I have no qualms whatsoever about using him."

He sounded like a coach who was planning to use his number three quarterback. Somehow, it never came about. The 49ers were a .500 team in '66, but Christiansen hoped to get them back in contention and he stuck with Brodie most of the way. If desire counted, Billy would have been in there every play.

By the time the final game rolled around, Bill Kilmer had seen a total of ten minutes and seven seconds playing time, appearing in just three ballgames. With the club going nowhere, some of the local sportswriters were getting restless.

One noted how Kilmer never left Christiansen's side during the ballgames, as he tried to get as close to the action as he could. The writer noted that "his (Kilmer's) burning desire to play, coupled with Christiansen's refusal to let him do so, except infrequently, made for a pathetic frustration."

And the same man added a sentiment shared by many Bill Kilmer fans. "This has been a horrible year for Billy Kilmer. Hopefully, it will be the last. Since they have so little use for him themselves, the 49ers should trade him. Kilmer has the ability to be a top hand for another club."

That's tremendous confidence in a man who hadn't even quarterbacked from the T formation for a full period in six seasons. But Billy Kilmer is the kind of guy people believe in. That became evident early in 1967. The National Football League was expanding once more and a new franchise was being added in New Orleans. As with all expansion teams the Saints, as they were called, wanted some solid veteran players around whom to build a respectable club.

Looking over the crop of back-up and veteran quarterbacks, the Saints quickly made their first choice. They picked Billy Kilmer.

There was no doubt about Bill's reaction. He was happy that he'd finally have a chance to play ball, even though the Saints were an expansion club, a place where the quarterback is often not much more than a glorified punching bag. But he was confident and defiant.

"I'm not afraid of being hit, so you won't find me looking for the ends, tackles, and linebackers when I drop back to pass. I'll be looking for my receivers. If you start worrying about the guys who are coming after you, then you might as well just run away and hide.

"This is the chance I've been waiting for. The 49ers used me in one exhibition game a year. They had no room for me and I wanted to go someplace where I could play. That's all I ever wanted, a fair opportunity."

There were others who expressed confidence in Kilmer, men who knew what the game was all about. One was Y. A. Tittle, himself traded by the 49ers when Kilmer and the shotgun came on the scene in 1961. Y. A. went on to set records and win championships with the New York Giants. By 1967, he was retired and a special quarterback consultant for the 49ers.

Speaking before a banquet audience in New Orleans, the old quarterback talked about the new Saints and about Billy Kilmer.

"I'm sure you're all going to be very pleased with Kilmer," Y. A. said. "He's the Bobby Layne type of quarterback not a picture passer, but Layne wasn't, either. All Layne did was beat you.

"Kilmer has a fine touch, is an outstanding leader and has an extraordinary knowledge of the game, more so than most quarterbacks. Kilmer played behind John

Brodie and George Mira at San Francisco, but there were times when some of us thought that maybe our best quarterback was sitting on the bench.

"It won't surprise me to see Bill become an outstanding quarterback here. He has the potential. He's had it for a long time."

By the time the exhibition season started, the Saints had picked up another quarterback, Gary Cuozzo, who had been an impressive back-up to John Unitas at Baltimore. Cuozzo was a standard dropback passer with a good arm. The only question was could he stand the gaff of playing behind an expansionist line?

Saints coach Tom Fears decided to alternate the two quarterbacks in the exhibition season. In the first game against the Rams, Cuozzo started and Kilmer relieved. The Saints lost, but Billy was outstanding in defeat and Fears named him the starter against St. Louis the following week.

As a starter, Bill immediately got the team moving. The line fired out at the snap, and the backs hit the holes, taking Kilmer's crisp handoffs. He was a fine field leader and moved the team well. But it was his passing that surprised everyone. As Y. A. Tittle had said, his passes weren't pretty, but they were getting there and the Saints had a couple of receivers who could hold onto the ball.

On two occasions, his passes found their mark in the end zone for scores and the Saints had a surprising, 23-14, victory. This set the pattern for the remainder of the exhibition season. Kilmer started with the first unit, with Cuozzo relieving. It was becoming apparent that Billy was winning the number one job.

Two more surprise victories followed. Then the Saints came up against the 49ers—a game Billy had been looking to with anticipation. It was played at Portland, Oregon, with many San Francisco fans on hand. Most of them remembered Kilmer well.

And if they didn't, he let them know who he was in a hurry. The first time the Saints had the ball they began moving. With veteran Jim Taylor at fullback, Kilmer had a professional ball carrier to work with. He mixed his running plays with short and swing passes to the sideline, and the 49er defenders seemed confused.

With the ball at the San Francisco 25, Kilmer faded back again. This time he spotted flanker Walt Roberts streaking for the end zone. He fired a wobbler, but as Roberts crossed the goal line the ball was waiting for him and he grabbed it for a score.

In the second quarter, Kilmer led two more drives. The first carried to the four. The 49ers packed in tight, expecting a running play. But Kilmer rolled right, then flipped a short pass to Taylor for another score. Later he called an end around to rookie John Gilliam who bolted in from five yards out.

When Billy gave way to Cuozzo in the second half, he had completed 13 of 19 passes for 126 yards and two scores. And he'd given the Saints a 21-3 lead. His ball-control game helped keep the pressure off the New Orleans defense, and when the club won, 24-10, much of the credit belonged to Billy Kilmer.

"Billy did one fine job for us," said Coach Fears. "It isn't easy to take a team in the first drive of the game, but he did it with a real professional effort."

As for Billy, he said simply, "I loved it. It was real sweet. But don't forget, they'll get a chance to even things up when we meet again in October." He wasn't about to say anything that would inflame the 49ers and give them something to shoot for later. In that way, Bill was smart, too.

By the end of the exhibition season, the experts

couldn't believe their eyes. Bill Kilmer had led the expansionist Saints to five straight victories. In those games he had fired for nine touchdowns, six more than Cuozzo. And with the possible exception of the veteran Jim Taylor (who had played his college ball at Louisiana State before starring with the Packers), Kilmer was the most popular player on the new team.

Fears had not yet named his starting quarterback, but most observers were rooting heavily for Kilmer.

"It's the feeling down here that Kilmer ignites the team when he gets into the game," wrote one newsman. "He's unorthodox and the players believe in him no matter what he tries. This is evident even in practice."

If the exhibition victories were a pipe dream, the regular season turned into a nightmare. Billy opened at quarterback and played steady ball. But the Saints as a whole were making too many mistakes, something not uncommon for new teams. When it really counted, they found victories hard to come by. Three games and three losses, and Billy suddenly found himself on the bench.

"It was hard to take," he confessed. "I knew I could move this type of team better than Gary (Cuozzo), but we were losing and the coach had to see what some of the other guys could do."

Sitting the bench was Bill Kilmer's idea of Hades. It ate him up inside. Cuozzo didn't fare much better and Fears began alternating his signal-callers much as he did in the exhibitions. In the final home game with Atlanta Billy came off the bench in the second half to rally his club to a 27-24 victory over the two-year-old Atlanta Falcons.

He got the starting call again in the final regular season game against the Redskins in Washington. With the pressure on, Billy responded, leading the team as he had in the preseason. He moved his runners well, mixed his plays, and tossed a pair of touchdown passes, one an 80-yarder to rookie Dan Abramowicz. The Saints won it, 30-14, and although he didn't know it at the time, Billy Kilmer had won himself a regular job.

The Saints finished with a 3-11 mark, a realistic figure for a first-year club. As for Billy, he'd had more opportunity than ever before, connecting on 97 of 204 passes for 1,341 yards and six touchdowns. His passing percentage was low at 47.5, but considering the circumstances, no one complained. He also finished as the team's third leading rusher with 142 yards on 20 carries. That's an average of 7.1, although he was running mainly on scrambles and broken plays.

By the following summer, Fears made his decision. He shipped Cuozzo off to Minnesota and told Bill he'd be going with him at quarterback. It marked the first time in his career that Bill Kilmer came to camp knowing he had himself a steady job.

"It's a great feeling to know you've finally got it made," said Bill to reporters. "Because I've had the chance to throw more in the last years, my arm is stronger than ever. Now the receivers know my passes better. There's a certain oneness forming throughout the team.

"We're all aware of the second-year lull like Atlanta experienced (the Falcons went from 3-11 to 1-12-1), but I'd say it's possible for the Saints to win 10 games this season." As usual, Billy was the eternal optimist.

Dave Whitsell, a veteran defensive back who had come to the Saints from the Chicago Bears, was also pleased to see Kilmer tabbed number one, and he told why.

"If Bill Kilmer decided to jump off a building, everyone here would jump with him," Whitsell said. "That's the kind of leader he is.

"I really think he's arrived. In fact, he's just a step away from greatness. I think he'll be the next Bobby Layne. He's got everyone around here thinking like winners. Layne did that, too."

It may have sounded like a lot of talk about a player who hadn't done much on the field. But in an early scrimmage against the San Diego Chargers, Billy showed his critics with a 14-of-22 day, good for 274 yards and three touchdowns. There was no longer much doubt about his ability to handle the T.

Several weeks later the Saints hosted the powerful Cleveland Browns in an exhibition game held before 70,045 fans at the Sugar Bowl in New Orleans. Kilmer turned them on again, connecting on 20 of 33 passes for 261 yards and two scores as the Saints routed the Browns, 40-27.

It wasn't an easy year. There were high points in the regular season, too, but a young team cannot pick up experience overnight. The Saints rolled over the Browns in that 40-27 exhibition, but when it counted during the year, Cleveland prevailed twice, 24-10, and 34-17.

The Saints were in the Century Division of the Eastern Conference during 1968, and, along with Cleveland, were joined by the Cardinals and Steelers. They lost to the Cards twice, but beat the Steelers a pair and actually finished higher than Pittsburgh in the standings. It was a 4-9-1 year for Coach Fears' club.

Billy was good, but not great. He suffered a hairline fracture of the ankle midway through the campaign. He missed the better part of three games—most players would have missed half a season.

There were some heroics for the home fans, but

some low moments, too, when the Saints' offensive line couldn't keep the opposition out of the backfield, or when one of Bill's passes was off the mark and intercepted. Yet he still compiled the busiest year of his career, throwing 315 times, completing 167 for 2,060 yards and 15 touchdowns. His passing percentage was over 50, at 53.0, and he was intercepted 17 times.

It's hard to say whether the Saints' fans and management expected miracles, but as Kilmer began leading the team through the 1969 season, a slow chorus of jeers began greeting the quarterback. The jeers increased at each home game. Fans began chanting for a little-known youngster named Edd Hargett, who had played his college ball at Texas A & M.

Yet Kilmer was in the midst of his finest season to date. True, there were some off days, but everyone has off days, and with a three-year-old franchise, it's bound to happen even more.

There was a bad game against Philadelphia in which Bill was yanked out in the middle. But the next week, he went wild against the St. Louis Cardinals. It seemed that every time he got the ball he threw for a touchdown. Cards' QB Charley Johnson was hot, too, and both clubs marched up and down the field all afternoon. When it ended, Kilmer and the Saints had come out on top.

Billy had thrown the ball 32 times, completing 22 for 345 yards and six touchdowns. Johnson also threw for six scores (a record for two quarterbacks in one game), but Billy got one on the ground, also, and his club won, 51-42. It was the Saints' first win of the year.

The victory augured well for the second half of the year, but Billy Kilmer would again have to call on all his courage and guts to continue leading the club.

In a game against his old teammates, the 49ers, Billy

suffered a severely separated left shoulder. He led the Saints to another win, 43-38, but after the game the doctors gave him the bad news.

"You need an immediate operation or the injury could lead to a permanent deformity of the shoulder."

"Can I play with it?" Kilmer asked.

"Yes, it won't get worse. But you know the consequences if you delay surgery."

"I'll play," said Kilmer without a moment's hesitation. When you wait as long as Billy Kilmer to be number one, you don't think about consequences.

Doctor Kenneth Saer, the Saints' physician, explained the injury to reporters. "It was a complete separation," said Dr. Saer. "It was the type of injury that required immediate surgery or could produce a painful joint. Without an operation he will have a deformity. His left shoulder will drop down and the clavicle (collar bone) will stick up."

It didn't matter to Kilmer. He continued to play, despite the painful shoulder and equally painful jeering from the fans.

A few weeks later, Billy started against the Steelers. Pittsburgh went ahead, 14-0, and the fans began chanting, WE WANT HARGETT! Fears paced the sideline, debating whether to make a change. Suddenly Bill got hot, hitting seven straight passes and culminating the drive with a touchdown strike to end, Ray Poage.

At the half, Billy had completed nine of 14 for 148 yards. But the patchwork offensive line had allowed him to be sacked five times for a loss of 56 yards. The Steelers still led at the outset of the fourth quarter, 24-27, and Fears finally sent Hargett into the game. The fickle fans went wild, cheering the youngster as Kilmer walked slowly and sadly to the sideline.

Hargett led a drive downfield. With the ball near the

goal line, Kilmer suddenly reentered to a shower of catcalls. Hargett had been shaken up and they wanted Bill's experience near the goal line. Sure enough, he set up the tying score and later the winning field goal. At the end his stats read 15 of 28 for 219 yards. Not bad. Asked about being pulled and the subsequent boos he heard, Bill was slightly angered.

"It's the coach's decision as to who plays and who doesn't. I'm just happy I made a contribution. As for the booing, it doesn't bother me normally, but it did a bit today because I thought I did a pretty good job."

There were additional victories—over the Eagles (26-17), and New York Giants (25-24)—giving the Saints a 5-9 mark and continued improvement, but Billy began feeling his days were numbered.

Statistically, he had his best year, completing 193 of 360 for 2,532 yards and 20 big touchdowns. Yet when the 1970 season opened, he found himself a part-timer, alternating with Hargett. There was increasing talk that the Saints were anxious to draft Mississippi's all-American, Archie Manning, and they were playing as though they wanted that last pick. After three years of progress, the Saints plummeted to a 2-11-1 mark. Wholesale changes were in order.

Billy threw just 237 passes that year, with six touchdowns to his credit against 17 interceptions. The high point of the season came in early November when he led the club to a 19-17 upset of the Detroit Lions, passing to Al Dodd in the closing seconds to set up Tom Dempsey's record-setting 63-yard field goal. But soon after the year was out, word began spreading that Kilmer would be traded.

"I asked out," said Billy, "as soon as they grabbed Manning in the draft. Where to go was another problem. I knew I couldn't go to a team with a youth move-

ment in progress. By the time they were contenders I'd
be too old to play anymore. I wanted my chance with a
winner, a team ready to make a move on the championship."

The Washington Redskins was not one of those
teams. The Skins were perennial losers. They had hired
the great Vince Lombardi in 1969 and his coaching ex-
pertise and leadership moved the club to a 7-5-2 season. But Lombardi's untimely death set the Skins back
and they were 6-8 in 1970. It looked as if they were
starting all over again.

Then the Redskin owners signed George Allen, the
fine coach of the Rams. Newsmen asked Allen what his
building program for the future would be.

"The future is now," he snapped in a now famous
statement. "I plan to make changes in this club before
the season starts. I want proven players and I'll trade
draft choices to get them. No rookie is going to pick up
experience at my expense."

Allen was true to his word. He was at the helm a little over two weeks when he made his first deal. He sent
a second stringer named Tom Roussel to New Orleans
in exchange for Billy Kilmer. Allen told the press that
Kilmer was a gutty leader who never quit, the type of
player he'd want no matter where he was coaching.

But wait a minute. Didn't the Redskins have a quarterback, a man named Christian Adolph "Sonny" Jurgensen? Right! And wasn't he regarded as one of the
greatest passers who ever lived? Right again. While Kilmer was having his big year in 1969, all Jurgy was
doing was completing 274 passes in 442 attempts for
3,102 yards, 22 touchdowns, and a completion percentage of 62.0. That's the kind of thrower Sonny was.
But he was also 37 years old and Allen wanted insur-
ance.

"I wasn't very happy about going to the Redskins," Kilmer confessed. "There was no way I could step in and beat out Sonny for the starting job. I couldn't see myself as a backup again, not at this point. A couple of years as a backup again and people would forget about me. I saw myself on this team, but with my chance— my real chance—never coming."

Bill's fears seemed justified, at least by Allen's other statements immediately following the trade.

"Sonny Jurgensen is still my quarterback," said the coach with finality. "This deal has nothing to do with Sonny's status here. We got Billy as a backup, a backup who could step in and do the job if he has to. When you get a guy like Kilmer it's better than having a draft pick."

Bill did a great deal of soul-searching during the off-season. But he had faith in Allen and there was just one way he could play it. When he reported to camp, he was in shape and ready to go.

During camp, reporters looked for an intense rivalry between the two quarterbacks, and some were surprised when they became fast, close friends. Both QB's looked good in camp, with some saying Kilmer had the edge in moving the team. Then before the first exhibition, Jurgy bruised a thumb and Kilmer started against the San Diego Chargers.

Bill was still learning a new system and didn't look good. The Chargers won the game and one George Allen streak was ended. His teams had never lost in the preseason. Jurgy was healed the next week and he saw most of the action in the ensuing games. When Kilmer did play, he continued to look nervous and unsure, and a familiar chorus of boos began cascading down from the upper reaches of Robert F. Kennedy Stadium in Washington.

Then in the second to last exhibition, the Skins were in Miami facing the Dolphins. Jurgy wasn't having a good game. In the third quarter he tossed one over the middle that was picked off by safety Dick Anderson. An angered Jurgy forgot about an unwritten rule that the quarterback protect himself. He tore after Anderson and blasted through several blockers to help with the tackle. When he got up he was in obvious pain.

Jurgy came slowly to the sideline, his left shoulder slumping lower than his right. A bone in the shoulder had been fractured. Sonny was through for at least eight weeks.

Suddenly and unexpectedly there was another quarterback in the game for Washington. The first time the Skins got the ball he dropped back and rifled a 47-yard scoring pass to Roy Jefferson. Miami won the game, but Bill Kilmer quickly showed his club he was ready to assume leadership.

"When I finished that game," Kilmer recalls, "George called me in just to tell me the job was mine. He wouldn't make any more moves. He also told me how much confidence he had in me. Here's my chance, I thought. Now there'd be no more talking or thinking. I just had to go out there and do it."

To the press, Bill confidently announced, "I can win and operate as efficiently as Sonny. If I didn't think that way I wouldn't be doing much good for the team."

Many observers agreed. Said one long-time Redskin booster. "Kilmer is perfectly suited for the Redskins. He'll win with them. He controls the game, but unlike Sonny, doesn't dominate it. He inspires. He relates. And he knows his limitations."

Through several other shrewd deals, Allen had given Kilmer a much-improved team with which to work. The offense was fine, with super-runner Larry

Brown and rugged Charley Harraway. Charley Taylor, Roy Jefferson, and Jerry Smith formed a first-rate trio of pass catchers. Both lines and the defensive linebackers and secondary were bolstered by the acquisition of able veterans, some aging, but all experienced and all winners.

The 1971 season opened in St. Louis with the Redskins coming to town as decided underdogs. Billy was deluged with a host of questions, most of them asking how he was going to fill Sonny Jurgensen's shoes.

"I'm not here to fill anyone's shoes," he snapped. "I'm here to follow a game plan and bring us home a winner."

It was a rainy, muddy Sunday as the Skins went up against the Cards. With the slippery football a risk to handle, Bill played it smart, sticking with basic running plays and only throwing occasionally. But one of his passes was a 31-yard touchdown strike to Smith and the Skins went on to win, 24-17. Allen said Bill called a "masterful" game and he exhorted the team to continue winning.

Critics said Bill threw just six passes and didn't really prove anything, so a week later he went out and shut some mouths. He did it at the expense of the Giants, in one of the most brilliant passing days of his career. He connected on 23 if 32 attempts for 309 yards. Two of his tosses went for TD's, both to Charley Taylor, one covering 71 yards, the other, two yards. He did it long and he did it short, as the Skins won, 30-3.

Suddenly the booing stopped. When the team came home, Kilmer was treated like a long-lost native son, an instant hero. And he didn't let them down. The next week he engineered a brilliant, 20-16, upset of the champion Dallas Cowboys, uncorking a 50-yard scoring toss to Jefferson to break the back of a Dallas rally.

With Kilmer at the helm, the Skins had become bona-fide contenders.

He made it four in a row the next week, leading his club to a 22-13 win over Houston, and the following Sunday he did it again, spearheading a 20-0 whitewash of St. Louis. The Skins were 5-0 and Billy Kilmer was riding high. Things were going so well with the surprising Redskins that some suggested the team might not be as successful if Jurgensen were playing. But the first to come to Sonny's defense was Bill Kilmer. He'd been there before.

"I say that we'd be doing even better if Sonny were playing. He's a winner who happens to be a fine person and great quarterback."

When someone suggested that Bill was being too modest, he replied promptly. "I'll never get a big head. I know as well as anyone that this kind of success lasts only as long as you win. But I'll say this much. I've never had an offense like this before. It's sensational. Coach Allen is building a club with an amazing amount of spirit. I just love being a part of it."

The bubble burst the next week as the Skins fell victims to the tough Kansas City Chiefs, 27-20. After a victory over New Orleans and a surprise 7-7 tie with Philadelphia, Allen's club lost two more to the Bears and Cowboys. The Dallas game ended 13-0, and Kilmer was getting down about his performance.

But the team pulled out just in time. They won two more and then traveled to Los Angeles to face the Rams. Early in the first quarter Kermit Alexander intercepted a Kilmer aerial and galloped 82 yards for a touchdown return that gave L.A. a 7-0 lead. Right there it looked as if Kilmer and the Skins would fold.

But a few minutes later Kilmer dropped back to pass, totally undaunted by the interception, and whipped a long one down the right sideline to Roy Jefferson. The ball was right on the button, and Jefferson gathered it in and continued on his way to a 70-yard touchdown.

Later in the period Kilmer connected with Clifton McNeil on a 32-yarder, and just before halftime he went for it on a fourth and one, in close, calling on Larry Brown who bulled over to give the Skins a 24-10 halftime lead.

Another TD strike to Jefferson highlighted the second half and when it ended the Redskins had won the game, 38-24. As for Kilmer, he had completed 14 of 19 passes for 246 yards and three touchdowns. Bill played down his performance, but the Associated Press thought enough of it to name him the Offensive Player of the Week.

Cleveland whipped the Skins the final week of the season, but Washington surprised with a 9-4-1 record, the best in 29 years, and entered the playoffs by having the best second-place mark in the NFC. Dallas captured the divisional crown at 11-3.

The first playoff game with San Francisco was a complete disappointment. The Skins fought hard, but were outgunned in the final quarter and beaten, 24-20. It was a double disappointment to Kilmer; the 49ers had been his first team. But the defeat couldn't cloud the Skins' amazing season. Allen himself said, "It was Bill Kilmer who brought us to the playoffs."

And a Washington newsman put Kilmer's performance into an even better perspective.

"Billy Kilmer did his job with a consistency that no one could have possibly predicted. He beat teams with his arm, with his head, and with his guts. He used everything at his command. He played the 1971 season with the candor of a street fighter. He would not lose. He would have to be beaten."

Statistically, Billy completed 166 of 306 passes for 2,221 yards and a 54.2 percentage. He tossed for 13 touchdowns and had an equal number of passes picked off. His teammates voted him Most Valuable Redskin and he finished fourth in the balloting for NFL Player of the Year. He was third in passing among all NFC quarterbacks.

In late January of 1972, Billy Kilmer won another award. He was voted the Most Courageous Athlete of 1971 by the Philadelphia Sports Writers Association. Bill was cited for coming back from his serious leg injury suffered in the auto crash, then overcoming other serious injuries to get the Redskins into the playoffs.

In his acceptance speech, the emotional Kilmer expressed his gratitude, then said he was going to give the award to someone in his family who deserved it more—his 12-year-old daughter, Kathy.

Kathy Kilmer was born with cerebral palsy and disjointed hips, and the little girl had undergone a series of operations to help her walk. When Billy received the award Kathy was facing still another operation and he had her on his mind. He was well aware that there were some things in the world more difficult than facing mammoth onrushing linemen.

When Billy reported to camp for the 1972 season he still didn't have the secure feeling that many pro quarterbacks enjoy. He had finished a strong number one, but Sonny Jurgensen was back, recovered from his injury, in shape, and ready to battle for his old job. Allen stated publically that he'd go with the quarterback who had brought the team to the playoffs, but Billy and everyone else knew that if Jurgy was right, he couldn't be denied indefinitely.

As for the competition, the two quarterbacks had only good things to say about each other.

"Billy's a fine quarterback," said Sonny. "He knows the position and he's a leader. We try to help each other and this competition can only make us better."

Kilmer's comment was, "Sure, Sonny wants to play as much as I do. It (the competition) will help us because each of us can move the club. We're the same that way. He's the better passer, but we move the club in different ways. There's no animosity between us. We could split the team up if we let it become an unfriendly thing. Winning is the objective, not who's going to play."

But it was a defensive back, Mike Bass, who perhaps came closest to characterizing the two quarterbacks. Bass was talking about the qualities of both men, then he added: "On third and ten I'd rather have Sonny, but on third and two, I'll take Kilmer."

Early in the exhibition season the Skins faced the Denver Broncos. Kilmer played the first half, hit six of 17, including a TD to Jefferson. He put 17 points on the scoreboard. Jurgy then took over and did even better, hitting six of seven for 144 yards and two TD's, including a 65-yard bomb to Tommy Mason. He, too, put 17 points on the board, and after the game George Allen said:

"No team in football has two better quarterbacks than we have."

Both continued to impress right through the season opener in Minnesota when Allen, true to his word, started Billy Kilmer.

In a hard-fought struggle from start to finish, the Redskins were outplayed statistically by the Vikings, but did enough things right to win, 24-21. The next week the team came home to face the Cardinals and

when Kilmer came out on the field he received a familiar reception—a chorus if boos. It seems the fans felt
in their hearts that a healthy Jurgensen should be the
team's quarterback. There were even bumper stickers
which called for Sonny's reinstatement.

Against the Cards Kilmer had an average game, yet
won, 24-10. Now there was a real clamor for Sonny in
Washington sports circles. Even Billy was forced to
comment on the growing issue.

"Let's face it," he said. "There has to be a clear-cut
number one for the team's sake. Sometimes a quarterback sees something in the first half that he knows he
can exploit in the second half. You can only get the
real tempo of the game by going all the way. I'm sure
Sonny would say the same thing."

Game number three was played against the lowly
New England Patriots in Foxboro, Massachusetts. Billy
was good that day. He threw three scoring passes and
just missed a fourth when Jefferson was ruled out of
bounds after an apparent touchdown catch. But the Patriots didn't quit and they somehow pushed over a late
score to upset the Skins by a point, 24-23. Two days
later Sonny Jurgensen was practicing with the first unit.

"I knew the day we lost a game I'd be replaced,"
said Kilmer after Allen announced that Jurgy was returning to the starting spot. "When you don't win,
you're replaced; it's as simple as that. I thought I had
my best game of the year against the Patriots.

"I'm not bitter with the Washington fans. Sonny is a
great quarterback and they want to see him, just as Jet
fans want to see Namath. But I felt I was doing the
job." Then he added, "Sonny deserves a chance to
play. I've just got to prepare myself as if I were the
starter, because you never know what will happen."

Like most great quarterbacks, Jurgensen made the

most of his opportunity. He led the Skins to two easy victories, showing that his classic passing form hadn't rusted with inactivity. He was hitting better than ever and it began to look as if Kilmer would never get in again. Then the Skins rolled into Yankee Stadium to play the Giants.

Jurgensen started and ran the offense for 13 plays. On the 14th, he called a little rollout to the right, took the snap and about four steps. Suddenly he pulled up lame, hobbling around in pain. Jurgy had ruptured his achilles tendon. Just like that. He walked slowly to the sideline, finished for the season once more. And without warning, Billy Kilmer was on the field, this time to stay.

Rising to the occasion despite his two-week layoff, Billy threw for two scores and Larry Brown rushed for an incredible 191 yards, as the Skins won the game, 23-16.

The next week, Billy showed everyone that he could do the job again. Facing Joe Namath and the New York Jets, Billy threw a 45-yard TD strike to Jefferson, a 70-yard completion to Taylor, setting up another score, and an 89-yard pass-run TD play to Larry Brown. The Skins won, 35-17, with Kilmer the star once again. After the game, Bill told newsmen how Jurgy's injury enabled him to change his style.

"I was throwing a lot stronger today than if Sonny was there behind me. Then I wouldn't take chances. Without him I can gamble because my position is different psychologically. Without him behind me I can freewheel out there and do things without worrying about the coach jerking me. My guys had confidence they could beat them deep and we did.

"It's just a different thing now knowing the job is mine. If Jurgy's there I might hold back and not zip the ball as hard—or maybe even run instead of throwing. But even if I throw an interception now, I stay in. Period."

In the ensuing weeks, Kilmer led the Skins as well as they'd ever been led. He whipped the Giants, 27-13, connecting on 15 of 23 for 256 yards, and he continued to win after that. In the five games that followed his return, Bill threw for 12 touchdowns, completing 54 of 95 passes for 859 yards.

During that same period the Skins were inside their opponents' 20-yard line 11 times. Billy Kilmer took the team in on all 11 occasions. In four of the five games, Billy brought the Skins from behind for the victory.

"Billy has improved tremendously over the last season," said Ted Marchibroda, the Skins offensive coordinator. "Somehow, last year, I got the impression that Billy didn't think he would stay here. He seems to just have more confidence now."

It was true. Kilmer led the club to six straight wins, seven including the Giant game when Jurgy was hurt. With an 11-1 record, the Skins clinched the Eastern Division title in the NFC. With 1,000-yard runner Larry Brown resting some minor injuries in the final two games, and the team already thinking ahead to the playoffs, the Skins dropped a pair and finished at 11-3.

Billy wound up fourth among NFC passers with 120 completions in 225 attempts for a 53.3 percentage and 1,648 yards. He threw for a big 19 touchdowns and had just 11 intercepted. It might not have been his best year statistically, but it had to be his most satisfying artistically.

Yet the season wasn't complete. There were still the playoffs, and the Skins wanted more than anything else to get into the Super Bowl. That was the goal everyone was pointing to.

Before the first-round playoff game against Green Bay, Billy Kilmer talked about the upcoming weeks.

"We've just got to dedicate ourselves, that's all," he said. "Just three weeks is all it will take, but we'll reap the value of that dedication for the rest of our lives.

Kilmer practiced what he preached against the Packers. He was a master of execution. Calling a tight, ball-control game, Billy had the Skins in command from the outset. With the score tied in the second quarter and the ball on the 32, Billy dropped back and lofted a perfect pass in the direction of Jefferson, who grabbed it on the goal line and went in. That made it 10-3, and the foot of Curt Knight gave the Skins the rest. Washington had a 16-3 victory and went into the NFC finals against Dallas.

Kilmer didn't throw much in the Packer game. He was just seven for 14 for 100 yards. But he did what was necessary. Larry Brown had 101 yards rushing and the two kept the Packer defense hopping.

What Kilmer did to the Cowboys the next week no one expected. Before a huge crowd at RFK Stadium, Kilmer and the Skins came out smoking. Billy had one of the most brilliant days of his career. He started it all with a 15-yard TD strike to Taylor in the second quarter, giving his team a 10-3 halftime lead.

Then in the final period he opened up, hitting Taylor with a neat 45-yard scoring pass to put the icing on the cake. Curt Knight had four field goals and the Redskins were NFC champs, 26-3, as their defense completely shut off the Cowboy attack.

Kilmer was 14 for 18, throwing for 194 yards in a display of passing and leadership that had the whole country talking. In the two weeks preceeding the Skins Super Bowl clash with Miami, everyone learned the

Billy Kilmer story. For the first time in his life he was a national celebrity.

The Super Bowl wouldn't be easy. Miami was bidding to become the first team ever to march through a pro-football season unbeaten in 17 games. They'd already won 16, the first 14 in the regular season and two more in the playoffs. Coach Don Shula had a well-balanced, deep, talented team. They seldom made mistakes, and they never let an opponent's mistake get by them.

The Dolphins feared the Skins and their tandem of Bill Kilmer and Larry Brown. Both had been spectacular in the Packer and Cowboy games.

"Billy Kilmer is what the Washington Redskins are all about," one newspaper story began. Another claimed that in reality Allen preferred Billy at quarterback to Jurgensen because of the way Kilmer stuck to a game plan and just chipped away at the opposition until they crumbled.

That's what he tried to do against the Dolphins. Playing in the Los Angeles Coliseum, where he had seen his first game so many years before, Kilmer tried to repeat his tactics of the other playoff games. He began by trying to establish his running game. It wasn't working. The stout Miami line was wrapping up Larry Brown before he could get started.

So Billy tried some short passes. He only had to throw a couple before he realized something. "I wasn't sharp. I wasn't throwing the ball well." And the Skins weren't moving.

Meanwhile, Miami quarterback Bob Griese was moving his team. In the first period he hit on six straight passes. The fourth pass was a 28-yarder to Howard Twilley that wound up in the end zone for a score. The kick made it 7-0.

The Skins tried to bounce back. Kilmer looked for Larry Brown midway in the second period, but middle linebacker Nick Buoniconti picked the ball off and returned it 32 yards. From there, the Dolphins drove in on the ground, Jim Kiick taking it over, and Miami had a 14-0 halftime lead.

The Skins worked desperately to score. But there was no running game and the Miami zone was laying for Kilmer. One time when Billy had Jerry Smith wide open in the end zone his pass hit the goal post and bounced away.

Not until late in the fourth quarter did the Skins score. And that was on a freak play. The Dolphins were trying a field goal, and a bad pass from center fouled the play. Cornerback Mike Bass picked up the football and raced it into the end zone. That made it 14-7, but there was next to no time left. Miami ran out the clock before the Skins could get the ball back.

It was a tremendous disappointment for everyone. Kilmer himself took the blame, saying he should have passed better. Maybe. But there was no running game to support him. Larry Brown had just 26 yards and that put the pressure on Kilmer. He was 14 for 26 but couldn't connect on the big ones or on the bombs. The Dolphin zone bottled him up.

Allen defended his quarterback. "He got us there," the coach said bluntly, and there was surely a bundle of truth in that statement. Kilmer had been the driving force of the Skins attack every since Jurgensen limped off the Yankee Stadium turf so many weeks before. Brown, Taylor, Harraway, Jefferson, and many of the other Redskins had outstanding years, but it was the spirit and leadership of Billy Kilmer that could be singled out.

What now for Kilmer? There aren't too many years

left. He's proved that he can play quarterback. He's shown he's a winner. He's taken his club to the Super Bowl.

But that's the one he didn't get. So Bill Kilmer will be back again and pitching. He may have to fight for his job. That's nothing new. One thing's for certain. Bill Kilmer will do anything he can to win.

Billy Kilmer once said that he never plans ahead. He's seen too many hopes, too many dreams dashed by some unforeseen occurrance. "Out of season I've never been a game-plan type of guy," is the way he put it.

No, he may not plan ahead. But no matter what happens, Bill Kilmer has proved time and again that he'll be ready to face anything.

TERRY BRADSHAW

It was a warm spring day in 1966. The Shreveport Woodlawn High School track team was engaged in a meet with a rival Louisiana school. The main body of the teams as well as most of the spectators were gathered around the oval track, watching the running and jumping events. Off in a far corner of the sprawling field a small group of people gathered for the javelin event.

The young competitors began hurling the spear for distance. Up stepped Shreveport Woodlawn's top thrower, a tall, lanky blond youth with a tough-looking, wiry build. He carefully adjusted his grip on the javelin, then stared straight ahead for a moment before starting his approach.

The big youngster ran with strong, powerful strides. As he neared the take-off line, he went into the final crossover and skip that characterizes perfect javelin form, then released the spear with a loud grunt.

All eyes followed the blue blur and it shot off his arm like a rocket. It seemed to keep rising as if jet propelled. When the other boys' throws began descending, this youngster's was still flying upward and outward. Finally, it began to arc downward. When it hit, its point buried deep in the ground so there could be no mistaking the spot.

Meet officials ran toward the fallen spear. They had not been standing out that far. Now they were excited. A tape measure was brought out. The distance was called off. They got another tape and measured again. Once more the distance was shouted out. Everyone began murmuring excitedly.

"Great toss, Terry."

"Way to chuck that thing, Ter."

"That showed 'em, Terry."

But even in the excitement of the explosive throw, no one quite realized exactly what happened. Terry Bradshaw had just broken the national prep school all-time javelin record with a toss of 244 feet, 11 inches. It beat the old mark by more than 13 feet.

Terry's teammates congratulated him and slapped him on the back. It was the first time that Terry Bradshaw's arm had brought him nationwide recognition, but it wouldn't be the last. Terry could have continued with the javelin and perhaps have become a world-class thrower. But he decided to concentrate on throwing something else, an oblong-shaped sphere made out of pigskin—a football.

Four years later, the same Terry Bradshaw would capture the national spotlight once again. And this time people other than a handful of track enthusiasts would know who he was. For in that span of time, Terry Bradshaw had honed his football talents to such a fine degree that he became the most talked-about pro football quarterback prospect since Joe Namath.

In Terry's case, it was a remarkable feat. While the

likes of Namath, Fran Tarkenton, Billy Kilmer, and later Jim Plunkett developed their football skills at great universities like Alabama, Georgia, UCLA, and Stanford, Terry Bradshaw got his gridiron baptism at Louisiana Polytechnic Institute.

What's that, you ask? Well, it's a relatively small university (student body about 8,000) located in Ruston, Louisiana. It plays its football in the Gulf States Conference against such teams as McNeese State, Lamar Tech, the University of Southwest Louisiana, and Northeast Louisiana State. The rest of the slate is similarly unexciting, except to football fans of the region and some footloose pro scouts.

Anyway, that's where Bradshaw played, but it wasn't long before the power attached to his right shoulder began speaking for itself. Anyone with an arm like Terry Bradshaw's would have attracted attention even if he played in no league at all.

A modern version of Jack Armstrong, the All-American boy, Terry was devoutly religious, clean-cut, and clean-living. He seemed to have the world at his feet when he broke a host of passing records at Louisiana Tech. Pro scouts were drooling, pro coaches dreaming . . . when they weren't scheming about ways to get him. With his bright blond hair and handsome face, he was truly a Golden Boy with a golden future.

Bradshaw said he was happy when the Pittsburgh Steelers drafted him, a team that had a 1-13 record the year before he got there. An impressive exhibition season solidified Terry's immediate claim to superstardom. The fans said that his release was quicker then Namath's, that he ran better than Tarkenton, that he was stronger than Gabriel. Perhaps no rookie quarterback in the history of the game has ever had so many words of praise heaped upon him at one time. But then the

1970 season started, and with it the most trying time of Terry Bradshaw's young life.

That life began on September 12, 1948, in Shreveport, Louisiana. Terry was the second of three sons born to Mr. and Mrs. W. M. (Bill) Bradshaw. When Terry was just a toddler, his family made a big move, going to Clinton, Iowa, where Mr. Bradshaw had taken a new job. Terry went through his early grammar school days there.

The Bradshaws remained in Iowa for a few years; then Mr. Bradshaw announced that he was taking the family back to Shreveport, where he became plant manager for the American Machine and Foundry Corporation. Years afterward, Mr. Bradshaw told why he did it:

"One reason I came back was because of sports. I wanted the boys to participate and I knew that Shreveport had a superior junior sports program."

Yet Bill Bradshaw adds a note of caution, lest someone misunderstand his intentions. "I never insisted my boys become athletes," he said frankly. "I hoped they'd be ballplayers, I exposed them to it and I encouraged them. But no one can force a boy into being something he doesn't have a real feeling for."

Terry's older brother, Gary, just a year his senior, was also a fine football prospect until a fall from a tree injured his back permanently. Craig, the youngest, is still only 15 years old. He has a possible future in baseball.

Bill Bradshaw was a sports lover from way back. When he was a kid he hung around with Joe Adcock (later the first baseman with the Milwaukee Braves) and the two were well-known figures on the Louisiana sandlots. When the Pittsburgh Steelers came to Shreveport for an exhibition game in 1952, somehow Bill

Bradshaw ended up driving their team bus out to the field. "They gave me $20 for that little ride," he recalls. "The most I ever got from other teams in those days was five dollars, so I've always maintained that the Steelers couldn't be a cheap outfit."

Of course, Bill Bradshaw had no way of knowing that his son would someday be negotiating with that same team, talking turkey at a figure considerably higher than the tip the elder Bradshaw received.

But despite his long association with sports and athletes, Bill Bradshaw was above all a devoted family man. A teetotaller and regular churchgoer, Mr. Bradshaw had always believed in family togetherness. The whole family often participated in after-dinner softball games.

"I always believed in keeping my boys busy," Mr. Bradshaw says, "either with sports or chores. That way, they wouldn't have time to get into trouble. In that respect, I guess I've been a strict father, but I don't feel I've been unreasonable, even though I always rode hard herd on the boys."

Mr. Bradshaw stuck by a set of firm rules. There were school night curfews for the boys, no smoking or drinking, respect for all elders, and no automobiles.

"I always had to know where my boys were," Mr. Bradshaw said, "and you don't know where in the world they are if they're running off in cars."

Though Mr. Bradshaw may seem tough and old-fashioned by today's standards, he stuck to his principles and his boys respected him for it. Right to this day, Terry has no complaints about his home life. In fact, he looks to the love and attention he had as a youth as one of the reasons for his success.

Terry's athletic career began slowly and quietly, but there were enough highlights along the way to indicate that there was something special about this bright youngster. When he was living in Clinton, Iowa, as a nine-year-old, he was picked by the coaches of the Little League to join an all-star team which was set to travel to New York. But Terry's joy quickly turned to disappointment when it was discovered that the boys had to be at least ten to make the trip.

When he was 13, he went to visit his grandmother in Coushatta, Louisiana, for two weeks. During that time he joined a local baseball team and promptly went out and pitched a perfect game. Even then he had the beginnings of that incredible arm.

By the time he entered junior high in Shreveport as a seventh grader, he was ready to play football. But he was small for his age and the coaches wouldn't even issue him a uniform. The next year he was bigger, but there were so many boys with experience that the team again ran out of uniforms before getting around to him.

It was a bitter disappointment for the youngster, but his father advised him not to give up, to believe in himself and keep at it. Then one day he and another youngster who didn't make the team were watching practice. Terry picked up an extra football and began throwing it to the other boy.

"I could throw pretty well, even then," he recalls, "and I told my friend to go out for some long ones. We threw for about 10 minutes or so and I guess the coaches noticed me, because the next day they gave me a uniform."

But that didn't mean they gave him the quarterback job. They made him a linebacker. "I loved it," says Terry now. "I remember one scrimmage when I really felt good. I think I must have made about a dozen unassisted tackles. I figured I had it made. But about a week later I broke my collarbone and missed the whole season."

The injury jinx continued to plague him. The next year, his last at Oak Terrace Junior High, the coaches made him the tailback in a shotgun-type offense, but he separated his shoulder before the first game and didn't return until the final two contests of the season.

"I threw about 50 passes in those two games," he remembers, "and didn't complete a whole lot, but it was a start."

When he arrived at Shreveport Woodlawn High the next year he was just starting to really grow. "I had a hard time convincing my Woodlawn coaches that I could play varsity ball," he says. "They thought I was too small at first, and even when I started growing I guess they still thought of me as a little guy. I rotated between the varsity and junior varsity in both my sophomore and junior seasons. I think I played in maybe three games with the varsity as a junior. They had a senior quarterback that year, Trey Prather (who later went to LSU and subsequently lost his life in Vietnam), who was breaking all the school passing records, and the coaches let him play as much as they could."

By the time he was a senior Terry could be denied no longer. What's more, the team had just one starter back and had to rebuild. Terry became the quarterback and immediately began firing bullet passes all over the field. With him at the helm, the Woodlawn Knights were winners again, taking the district championship and going all the way to the state finals before losing a tough one to Sulphur High, 12-9.

Terry was a dedicated football player by then, and knew he wanted to concentrate on the sport in college. He came home one day shortly after the season ended and told his father that he was going to forget about track that spring. Bill Bradshaw didn't like to hear that. Terry's arm had been getting stronger all the time and he was beginning to make his mark as a javelin thrower.

"There were two reasons why I wanted him to stick with it," says Mr. Bradshaw. "Naturally, I wanted him busy, but I also felt he had the ability to break the state record in the javelin and I wanted him to fulfill that potential. I asked him to stay on the team, to get that record for me. And that's the only time I ever asked one of my boys to actually do something for me. Terry was a good kid and he agreed."

In the second meet of the season, Terry tossed the spear 222 feet. That throw broke the state record his father had asked him to aim for. And, of course, he didn't stop there. Several weeks later at Bossier City he got off the big one, the toss of 244 feet, 11 inches that broke the national prep school all-time javelin record.

"I was really surprised at the number of cards and letters I got from track fans after breaking the record," he recalls. "There were even some from Europe. People were sending me things to autograph for them, and some guy in Italy even sent me a present. ... I could have had a track scholarship to almost any school in the country, but I knew then that it was time to concentrate on football."

The next problem was picking a college. The track offers were still much more numerous than the football feelers and Terry did not have very many schools to choose from. Finally, he narrowed it down to three schools, Baylor, Louisiana State University, and Louisiana Tech. The first two are big-time outfits where he could surely achieve national recognition. But there was something about Baylor he didn't like (some said it was the sight of whiskey bottles in many of the dormitory rooms), and things never worked out with LSU.

In fact, it was because the LSU people hemmed and hawed for so long that he finally decided on Tech, which was located some 70 miles from his home in Shreveport.

"As far as I'm concerned," Terry said in answering critics who felt he had made a mistake, "Tech plays a real good brand of football. They have a fine coaching staff, use a pro-style offense, and are playing in a new 25,000-seat stadium. If I'm good enough to play pro ball I'll get my chance, no matter which college I attend."

It didn't take Terry long to find admirers. He was just a freshman when a scout saw him for the first time. The man's name was Jim Palmer, and he worked for an organization called BLESTO-V, a talent scouting service which worked collectively for the Bears, Lions, Eagles, Steelers, and Vikings.

Anyway, Palmer watched the youngster throw a football for the first time and quickly filled out a report which read in part, "He has the best arm I've ever seen on a freshman quarterback."

Palmer returned in May, when Terry was in the midst of spring practice with the varsity. He was still a freshman, but the scout was already looking to next year. "This youngster has the quickest delivery and strongest arm I've ever seen on a sophomore." Then he added a negative note. "He doesn't scramble well and needs experience." What did anyone expect? Terry was still green behind the ears, though he had seen some varsity action as a frosh.

The club was young and inexperienced itself. Terry was the number two quarterback but didn't really see much action as a frosh in 1966. He was in long enough to throw 81 passes, completing 34 for a 42.0 percentage and 404 yards. He failed to throw a TD pass, however, and had three picked off. The club's 1-9 record and 83 points scored indicated its entire caliber of play.

After the season, Joe Aillet, Tech's coach of 26 years, retired, and Maxie Lambright took his place. Also coming with Lambright as an assistant was Mickey Slaughter, a former Tech signalcaller who played four years with the Denver Broncos of the American Football League. Terry always gives Slaughter much of the credit for his development.

"I built up my arm by lifting weights," he said, "a lot of weights. And plenty of throwing helped me, too. But, basically, it was Coach Slaughter who made me mentally tough. I may have had the physical ability when I first came to Tech, but I didn't have the confidence needed to make an offense go. Someone had to give me the drive and that's what Coach Slaughter did. He drove the confidence into me."

The confidence didn't come overnight. Terry was an alternate quarterback his sophomore year of 1967, as the team began rebuilding under Coach Lambright. The Bulldogs had a couple of big wins, 34-7 over Delta State, and 41-31 against Lamar Tech. But there were losses, too, including a season-ending 58-7 rout at the hands of Southern Mississippi. When it ended, the Bulldogs were 3-7. All they could do was hope their young players would come of age in '68.

As for Terry, he began to show the passing form that was to make him a national celebrity in less than two years. He threw the football 139 times, completing 78 for 981 yards and a 56.1 percentage. He fired his first three touchdown passes, but on the other side had 10 picked off. He still had to learn when to run and when to eat the ball.

When Terry returned for his junior year of 1968 he finally knew the quarterback job was his. He'd be calling the plays and running the Bulldog offense. And it wasn't long before he opened up. He was 13 for 30 and 216 yards in an opening victory over Mississippi State, 20-13. The next week he was a conservative, hitting on just eight of 15 for 105 yards and a score, as Tech whipped East Carolina, 35-7.

Then in the following two weeks, Terry really began putting on an aerial show. He was 20 of 38 for 319 yards and three scores against McNeese State, and then made the fans' eyes pop with a scintillating 28 of 47 for 432 yards and two scores against Southwestern Louisiana. Unfortunately, the Bulldog defense wasn't equal to the task, and Tech lost both games, 27-20 and 28-24. So when the club faced Northwestern State the following week, they were determined not to lose another.

"We figured the success of our season hinged on that game," said Terry. "Some people were calling us chokers, and rapping the defense. But let's face it, it's a team effort and everyone's to blame for a loss."

It was the 53rd meeting between the two teams, so if anyone is wondering how long these small Louisiana schools have been playing the grid game, there's the answer. Anyway, it was a wild contest all the way. Northwestern dominated the first half as Terry could complete just two of 12 passes in a performance that had people shaking their heads.

Tech had a 7-0 lead mostly on running plays, with Terry completing one 13-yard pass which brought the ball to the two. Minutes after the score, the Golden Boy was nailed in his own end zone for a safety, and a subsequent Northwestern score made it 9-7. It was a 19-7 game at the half and the Bulldogs looked like they were going down to a third straight defeat.

But in the third period, Terry began hitting. He found Tommy Spinks open for passes of 10 and 13 yards, then rocketed one to Larry Brewer in the end zone for a score. Northwestern upped its lead to 26-14 before Tech drove downfield again, with long runs by its halfbacks. Terry then took it over from the one and the kick made it 26-21. Another Tech score minutes later made it a 28-26 game, with the Bulldogs out in front once again.

Terry got a third TD on a sneak, but the Tech defense again weakened. The Demons scored twice to go ahead by 39-35 with less than three minutes left. Tech got the ball and Terry tried to start another drive. But when he tried a pass over the middle it was picked off by a State defender. With just 2:42 left in the game, it seemed that State had won.

Only this time the Bulldog defense held, and Northwestern was forced to punt. The kick by Larry Smith was returned a few yards to the Tech 18 by Butch Danile. Bradshaw re-entered the game with his team 82 yards from paydirt and just 25 seconds remaining. There was time for one play, perhaps two.

Terry took the snap and dropped straight back. Northwestern had its linemen charging and Bradshaw knew he didn't have much time. He waited until the last possible second, then fired hard and long over the middle. Flanker Ken Liberto ran under the ball at the Demon 40 and suddenly was in the clear, racing all the way to the end zone to complete the dramatic, 82-yard play. Louisiana Tech had won, 42-39.

As for Terry, he had returned from a disastrous first half to complete 11-of 15 second-half passes in leading his team to a great win. And the game turned the season around just as Terry had said it would. Tech went on to take its final five games. The Bulldogs finished with an 8-2 mark and the Gulf States Conference title.

Terry Bradshaw had rewritten the Bulldog record book. During 1968 he completed 176 of 339 passes for a whopping 2,890 yards. His completion percentage was 51.9 and he rifled 22 touchdown passes to his waiting receivers. Just 15 of his throws were intercepted.

Interestingly enough, five of those interceptions came in one game, against Northwestern Louisiana, and they served to show just what kind of a competitor Terry Bradshaw was.

On four of the five occasions it was Bradshaw who busted through blockers to make the tackle. And he hit the ballcarriers so hard that he broke the collarbone of one of them.

"I like the physical side of football," he admitted one day. "I like being hit. I've seen a lot of quarterbacks, even in pro ball, who seem quiet, almost passive on the field. When they get hit they just lie there. They don't even get mad. But when I get hit, I get very mad."

There were times at Tech when Coach Lambright had to send in messengers, not with plays, but with orders for Terry to cool it, to stop seeking out contact and to run out of bounds when he saw he'd be hit. The temptation to lower his head and plow into a defender was always great.

The season wasn't yet over for Terry and the Bulldogs. Their fine record earned them a bid to the Grantland Rice Bowl against Akron University. While the game didn't compare in glamor or importance to the Rose or Orange Bowls, both teams were nevertheless ready to give it everything they had.

It was a cold December 14 when the two clubs met at

Murfreesboro, Tennessee, but it didn't take long for Terry Bradshaw to warm up the air with his passing.

The Bulldogs began driving as soon as they got the ball. Bradshaw took them downfield by mixing his throwing with running plays and keepers. With the ball on the 16 he dropped back, then took off and scrambled by several Akron players for the score.

Minutes later he struck again, hitting Tommy Spinks with a 36-yard scoring pass, and before the quarter ended, Buster Herren banged over from the two, giving Tech a 21-0 lead.

Akron came back with touchdowns in the second and third quarters, making it 21-13, but in the final period Terry began hitting again, culminating one drive with a six-yard pass to Larry Brewer, and a second by scrambling over himself from the eight. Witnesses claim that he completed one pass after being hit by six different Akron players, with three still hanging onto him when he threw.

The final score was 33-13, and Terry Bradshaw won the Most Valuable Player Award hands down. He had completed 19 of 33 passes for 261 yards and two scores. In addition, he gained 71 yards on 12 running plays, though that statistic was modified by 36 yards lost trying to pass. But when he ran, he did it well.

After the bowl game Terry could sit back and watch the honors roll in. And there were many. He was the Player of the Year in the Gulf States Conference; the Most Valuable Player at Louisiana Tech; a first team all-America selection by the American Football Coaches Association; the Athlete of the Year in the Gulf States Conference as voted by the Louisiana Sports Writers Association.

That wasn't all. By the end of his junior year, Terry Bradshaw had become one of the most heavily scouted quarterback prospects in the country. At 6-3, 215 pounds, he had the size and strength to play in the pros, and no one ever questioned the quality of his arm.

When Terry returned for his senior year, it was like an anticlimax. What more could he do for an encore? He was already NCAA college division total offense leader (2,987 yards in 426 plays).

Terry had a multitide of laudatory nicknames, perhaps the most popular being "The Rifleman," given him for two reasons—his arm and his facial resemblance to actor Chuck Connors, who played in a TV series of that name. Indeed, his square-jawed, highcheekboned appearance, complete with a cleft in his chin, made him a very handsome football player.

And once the season opened, his opponents knew that success hadn't gone to Terry Bradshaw's head. He took up right where he left off—pitching strikes. Three TD's against East Carolina highlighted the opening win (final score: 24-6) and that was just the beginning.

In the third game against Southwestern Louisiana, Terry hit 15 of 25 for 207 yards and ran for another 68 on 10 tries to highlight an easy victory. Then in the fifth game against Chattanooga, Terry played barely one half, hitting nine of 10 for 209 big yards and three TD's. In fact, the stadium transformers failed and the game had to be halted for some 88 minutes. Some joked that it was Bradshaw's lightning that shortcircuited the lights. One pro scout on hand, John Carson of the Eagles, was really impressed by Terry's cool that night.

"I watched him throw a 20-yard touchdown pass and then all the lights went out," Carson said. "The place was dark for almost an hour and a half. When the lights came on again, Bradshaw came back onto the field and threw a 76-yard touchdown pass on the very first play. I couldn't believe how cool he was about it."

The whole season was cool. Tech lost just once, a 24-23 squeaker at the hands of Southern Mississippi. Included in their fine 8-1 record was a smashing 77-40 triumph over Lamar Tech, which broke several school and conference marks. Terry was 17 of 33 in that one, for a big 316 yards. The team returned to the Grantland Rice Bowl again in 1969, this time facing East Tennessee. That one was a mild upset. East Tennessee defenders overwhelmed the Bulldog line and rapped Terry 12 times for 143 yards in losses. He still managed to complete 20 of 39 for 299 yards, but Tech lost, 34-14.

Thus ended the college career of Terry Bradshaw. He wasn't quite as busy his senior year. Many games were won early and he managed some bench time. He nevertheless completed 136 of 248 for 2,314 yards and 14 scores. That gave him a career total of 463 completions in 879 attempts for a mammoth total of 7,149 yards. His passing percentage for four years was 52.7, and he fired away for 42 touchdowns.

This time his all-America honors weren't restricted to the small college division—although he copped all the top prizes in that division. He was a first-team selection of the American Coaches Association and *Time* Magazine, and made the second team in the *Sporting News* poll. And, of course, he was once again Gulf States Conference Athlete of the Year.

While Terry Bradshaw was rewriting the record books at Louisiana Tech, the wheels were turning elsewhere. The wheels that drive the huge complex known as the National Football League. The men who know football best had been watching Terry for some time already, and their comments were as splendid as Terry's best bullet pass.

Gil Brandt, chief scout of the Dallas Cowboys, didn't mince any words in talking about tall Terry. "He's tremendous," said Brandt. "He's got to be a first-round choice for sure. I think he'll be the first quarterback picked. In fact, it wouldn't surprise me if he was the first player drafted. Just look at what he has. He can really throw the football. He's got a real quick, accurate delivery. And he's strong with good speed."

The Cowboys' receiver coach, Ray Renfro, echoed the sentiment. "He's got to be the best I've seen this year. His arm is so strong that he doesn't have to have perfect balance when he's throwing. He could really fit into our system. It makes me sick to know we don't have a chance to get him." Renfro was aware that Bradshaw would be drafted long before the Cowboys' first chance to pick came around.

Then Brandt elaborated more, comparing Terry with some of the other top QB's who would be available in the upcoming draft.

"There are some real good quarterbacks available this year," the scout said. "Some people think Mike Phipps of Purdue is the best. Archie Manning of Mississippi is a good one, so is Bill Cappleman of Florida State. But to tell the truth, I'd take Bradshaw over any one of them. I just think he's a better football player.

"Of course, a guy like Phipps has that Big Ten experience. He's been in the Rose Bowl and has proven himself a winner. There's a big difference between that and playing in the Gulf States Conference. But Bradshaw has the greater potential.

"What it amounts to is that someone will have to make a decision like we did when we drafted Calvin

Hill out of Yale. They can take Bradshaw over Phipps and learn three years later if they were right."

The Colts' George Young watched Bradshaw in action several times and gave the youngster (and the team drafting him) his blessing.

"There's really no risk in drafting Bradshaw," he said. "He's tall enough, strong enough, and fast enough. He's got the arm and the intelligence. Add to that good poise, ability to avoid rushers, and a propensity to move a ballclub. What else do you want in a quarterback?"

Former Colt defensive back Carl Taseff, also scouting at the time, watched Terry fire one pass and said, "I've seen enough. Just look at the speed on the ball. And look at his hands. They're like ham hocks."

That was just a sampling. Former Giants' coach Jim Lee Howell called Terry a "big Sammy Baugh," and one-time quarterback great Y. A. Tittle said "they ought to charge admission just to watch him warm up."

The stage seemed set for a first-round draft. But just to show that he could play with the big boys, Terry accepted invitations to participate in The North-South Game and then in the Senior Bowl game, both postseason affairs that always attract the top college players and pro prospects in the country.

Terry journeyed to Miami for the North-South game that was set for Christmas Day. Mike Phipps was slated to start for the North team, and Terry would be battling Florida State's Bill Cappleman for the starting job on the South Side. The South's coach was Bill Peterson of Florida State, and that gave Terry an early line on just who the starter would be.

The scouts watched the practice sessions intently. When it began to look as if Cappleman would start for the South, Ace Parker of Duke, one of the BLESTO-V scouts, commented, "Look at Bradshaw's delivery! He's really impressive. Cappleman isn't nearly as quick as he is."

Another interested spectator at Miami was Chuck Noll, the youthful coach of the Pittsburgh Steelers. Pittsburgh had just completed a dreadful 1-13 season, the same as the Chicago Bears, and the two teams flipped a coin to see which would get the number one draft choice. The Steelers won. That meant Chuck Noll had a lot of quick decisions to make.

First of all, he wasn't sure if he wanted to draft a quarterback. He had played a rookie in 1969, Terry Hanratty of Notre Dame, a Pennsylvania-born lad who seemed like the right man to run the team in the 1970's. But Hanratty hadn't really impressed, so Noll still kept an open mind. He also had good reports on Phipps, San Diego State's Dennis Shaw, and Bradshaw.

"I had never seen Terry in person before I went to Miami," Noll recalls, "but the minute I saw him walk onto the practice field I thought to myself, 'He's an athlete.' Then I watched him begin throwing. I was really startled. I knew from the films that he had a strong arm, but film doesn't measure intensity. He really winged it in there."

Unfortunately, Terry suffered a hamstring pull that day and it slowed him down a bit. It also gave Peterson the final reason to start his own boy, Cappleman. Terry played part of the second and fourth quarters, and ran the team well. When someone asked him if the hamstring bothered him, Terry exploded, "Bull!" he said. "I didn't play more because the coach wanted Cappleman in there. Now I'm going to Mobile for the Senior Bowl and I'm going to beat him (Cappleman) out."

Back in Pittsburgh, Chuck Noll and his staff watched the game on television, then studied the films.

"We weren't convinced. Phipps hadn't done much, either, while Dennis Shaw had been the MVP of another all-star game, so it was still a three-way race."

In between the North-South and the Senior Bowl, Terry jumped into a lesser game that was covered by Steeler defensive line coach Walt Hackett. Hackett came back to Pittsburgh and brashly announced to Noll, "Bradshaw's the guy!"

By now, Noll was thinking more and more about drafting one of the quarterbacks, and he hopped a plane to Mobile five days before the Senior Bowl game.

The coaches timed the players in the 40-yard dash. Terry sprinted the distance in 4.7 seconds, very good time for quarterback. But in doing that, he pulled the hamstring muscle again and his coach, Don Shula, offered to let him sit the game out. Terry wouldn't hear of it.

"I went down to Mobile to beat out Cappleman, win the position, start, and have a good game. Nothing was going to stop me."

That's what really impressed Noll. He watched Terry in practice, setting up and throwing despite the injury, responding to top-flight competition like a pro.

In the game itself, Terry started and played very well, winging his passes with authority and hitting his receivers. In the third quarter he was hit hard and suffered two broken ribs. Yet he continued to play. The game ended in a 27-27 tie. Terry had completed 17 of 31 passes for 267 yards and two TD's, and was named the game's Most Valuable Player. Now the Steelers had settled on Bradshaw as the man. Their only remaining question was whether to trade him for established players, or make him their quarterback.

There were several things to take into consideration. First of all, many pro teams began making offers to the

Steelers even before the draft. "We've had some fantastic offers," was the way vice-president Dan Rooney of the Steelers put it. "We've got to assess them."

And Pete Retzlaff, the general manager of the Eagles and one of the men who admitted to making an offer, said, "O. J. Simpson might have gotten more publicity last year, but internally within the league, there's much more talk about Bradshaw. He's evidently a quarterback who can run your team, and run it right now."

That was a major factor. The other was the Steeler organization. It had a very bad history of getting rid of quarterbacks who later became superstars. Just listen to the list of throwers who began in the Pittsburgh organization and were shipped out before they could develop. It begins with Sid Luckman and from there moves to John Unitas, Earl Morrall, Jack Kemp, Len Dawson, and Bill Nelson. That's amazing. All of them became outstanding signalcallers. The Steelers didn't want that to happen again with Bradshaw.

On the other hand, the Steelers had to consider the quarterbacks who had previously been the number one choice of the entire league. The list reads like a who's-who of forgotten men—Boley Dancewicz, Harry Gilmer, King Hill, Randy Duncan, George Shaw, Terry Baker, Bobby Garrett, and Bill Wade. None of them made it. True, Paul Hornung was another first-choice quarterback, but he found his greatest success at halfback.

The Steelers tried to ignore all those factors. They just looked at Terry as a football player. With offers coming in right up to draft time, the Steelers made their decision. They picked Terry Bradshaw.

"I'm thrilled to death," was Terry's first reaction. "I had a hunch I might go high, maybe first round. But being the number one pick is the most exciting thing that's ever happened to me."

Now Terry had to negotiate his contract with the Steelers. Taking some advice from Roman Gabriel and his dad, Terry decided to do his own negotiating with help from a personal friend, a local attorney from Shreveport. He stayed away from the high-powered agents who had come into vogue about that time.

Slowly, he began to see himself within a much larger scheme of things.

"I was very happy to be chosen by the Steelers," he said. "I wanted to go to a losing team all along. That way, if the team became a winner they'd do it with me. From the first time I went to Pittsburgh and met some of the guys and the coaches, I knew the Steelers were a team in search of a leader. That's what I'm going to be paid for . . . to be a leader."

On one of his early trips to Pittsburgh, Terry went out for a night on the town with veteran linebacker Andy Russell. Terry asked Russell just how he thought the veterans would accept him.

"You'll probably get your share of needling," Russell answered.

The blond bomber bristled slightly. "Look," he told the vet. "I'm a leader. If anyone gives me trouble in the huddle—and I don't care who they are—I'm going to sting them."

Russell was impressed, just as everyone else was by the youngster's confidence. Before long he had signed his contract, a six-figure package, estimated in the $200,000 to $300,000 range. He was well satisfied. He was also beginning to reap the reward of being an instant "personality."

In February he went to New York to model for a picture layout in *Harper's Bazaar* magazine. The story was designed to show how women's fashions were influenced by sports. Other male models were rather well known, men like Arthur Ashe, Mark Spitz, and Bob Hope. But when it came to football, editor Gloria Moncouer wanted a new face.

"Joe Namath was too old, too overphotographed," she said. "As soon as I saw all the pictures of Terry Bradshaw in the papers I knew I wanted him. I wanted those blue eyes to show."

Terry described the whole experience as "exciting." Yet he is a man who never loses his sense of reality. Not even the instant celebrity treatment could change his basic nature.

Still a devout Baptist and already a longtime member of the Fellowship of Christian Athletes, Terry continued doing volunteer church work in the summer, acting as a youth director for underprivileged kids.

"I've always said that I'm a Christian who happened also to be an athlete," he once told a reporter. "Any time I have the chance to speak to kids I tell them that everyone isn't selected to be the same thing in life. Whether it's an athlete, or something else, you've got to accept it for what it is.

"I always figured it this way. It was the Lord who gave me this body and strong arm and if the arm went dead on me tomorrow, it would just be Him taking it back. I believe—and believe strongly—in God, and I don't think it's a cornpone thing."

So Terry was his own man and seemed to know where he was going. When he got to the Steeler camp, it soon became obvious that his main competition would be Terry Hanratty. The other quarterbacks, Dick Shiner and Kent Nix, would soon be on their way to other teams. Hanratty was less than impressive his rookie year of '69. He had trouble handling the big pass rush and hitting his receivers. He connected on just 52 of 126 attempts, a 41.3 average, for 716 yards and eight touchdowns. Thirteen of his passes were picked off. So the battle for the top job would be a wide-open affair between the two Terrys.

By the time the exhibition season rolled around, Coach Noll was alternating his two quarterbacks. Hanratty played the first and third quarter in the opener against the Dolphins, with Bradshaw relieving in the second and fourth. Miami won the game, 16-10, but it was Bradshaw, as usual, who did most of the impressing.

Blond Terry completed nine of 19 passes, with another five dropped by receivers not used to the velocity with which he threw. He engineered Pittsburgh's only touchdown drive.

"I wasn't really pleased with my performance," he said later. "I made a lot of dumb rookie mistakes and didn't do a good job of reading defenses."

Then Terry admitted that something happened in the huddle that he kind of expected. "On the second play of the second series I ran, they all came back yakking and laughing it up. I felt they were testing me, but it made me mad. As a rule I don't like to cuss anyone out, but this time I said, 'Let's cut out the damn fooling around and get down to business.' They were quiet for the rest of the time I played."

Miami coach Don Shula didn't agree with Terry's critical self-analysis. After the game the Dolphin mentor said, "I've been a Bradshaw man all along. He's tough and strong and has a great arm. Plus he's a remarkable athlete."

Chuck Noll agreed. He wanted to take a longer look at his rookie and played him all the way the next week against Minnesota. All Terry did was complete 12 passes and lead his club to a 20-13 victory. He was progressing right on schedule.

The following week the Steelers came into Pittsburgh for their first game in brand-new Three Rivers Stadium. They were facing old rivals, the New York Giants, and Terry once again had the nod as the starting quarterback.

This time he was really hot. Directing the Steeler offense like a 10-year veteran, he quickly got his club on the board with two early touchdowns. The second was a beauty, a 37-yard touchdown strike to rookie Ron Shanklin and the crowd went wild.

When Bradshaw came to the sideline to give way to Hanratty they screamed for his return, and they got him again in the second half, as he continued to lead his club to an easy, 21-6, win. Along the way he completed 15 of 23 passes for 244 yards, and he used his ground game very well to keep the young Giant defense off-balance. He was beginning to compile some impressive pro statistics.

"How far can a team go with a rookie quarterback?" Chuck Noll asked himself after the game. Then he answered his own question. "I really don't know. But this is a different kind of rookie."

Giants' quarterback Fran Tarkenton, who sat out the game with a pulled muscle, had plenty of time to evaluate Bradshaw's performance. "He's got a lot of ability and he's sure a good thrower," said Fran the Scram. "Still, it's too early to make a real judgement because he has so much to learn."

As for Terry, it was like a dream come true. "The new stadium . . . we won . . . my girl was there. It was all beautiful. I wasn't nervous at all today. I started seeing more things out there, especially my secondary receivers. I was looking and I was reading, and that's what it's all about."

Terry's girl was Melissa Babish, Miss Teenage America in 1969. They began dating in 1970 and were married in April of 1972.

As the season neared, Terry was brimming with confidence. "The way I feel," he told the press, "there isn't anyone in the world who can move this club like I can. Really, I can just feel it."

The pre-season statistics bore out his prediction. He had truly moved them more effectively than Hanratty. The team had won four straight exhibitions after the loss to Miami, including a convincing win over the rugged Oakland Raiders, and Terry was instrumental in every one of them. He completed 51 percent of his pre-season passes for 663 yards and three scores. His arm and running ability continued to impress people, and his confidence made everyone believe that the Steelers could win. It was a team that had not taken any kind of title in some 38 years and the fans were hungry. They could wait until the opener against Houston rolled around.

Besides Bradshaw, rookie Shanklin and Dave Smith gave the club two fine receivers, while John Fuqua and Preston Pearson were more than adaquate runners. Both lines were improving, but many of the young players lacked important experience. Still, many predicted a .500 year or better, which was quite optimistic in view of the 1-13 finish of the year before.

Bradshaw's goals were simple. "I want to be the greatest passer who ever played," he said. "I want to be the best quarterback in the game."

But there were some tough nuts to crack in the Oiler game. Terry would be throwing to three rookie receivers, and they'd be going against a very rough secondary. Terry wanted to strike fast. On the second play of the game he lofted a long pass toward Hubie Bryant. If he connected it would have been a touchdown. But he missed.

After that, everything seemed wrong. Either his passes were dropped by nervous receivers or they wobbled and missed their mark. Perhaps he was nervous, too. Shanklin got free in the second quarter, but the ball slipped off Terry's hand. Instead of a bullet, it was a floater, and the receiver had to stop and wait for it. Another sure touchdown went down the drain.

On the other hand, Houston was doing a nice job. Speedy Jerry Levias caught two TD passes and the Oilers had a 16-0 lead midway in the third period. Bradshaw's passes were still way off the mark, and Noll finally made a decision. He sent Terry Hanratty into the game. The hometown Pittsburgh fans were shocked to silence.

When it ended, Houston had won, 19-7, with Hanratty leading the Steelers to their only score. Bradshaw had had a miserable afternoon, completing just four of 16 for 70 yards. His brilliant exhibition season seemed like a memory from the distant past. Even he couldn't understand what happened.

"I felt so good out there," he said. "Then I did so poorly. I can't figure it out. All those people expected so much. I thought I was loose and relaxed, but nothing seemed to work."

The next week the team traveled to Denver. Terry was back at the helm for a second chance. Surely, it had just been a bad game, nothing more.

Statistically, the Denver game was better, but not the outcome. The Broncos won, 16-13, as Terry completed 13 of 26 passes for 211 yards. But none of his tosses went for scores. He came out of the game only when he was momentarily racked up by tackle Dave Costa—he was "getting his bell rung," as the pros say. But there were still a lot of mistakes.

Against Cleveland the next week Terry had a similar day. He hit on 13 of 29 for 207 yards, but he had three picked off and didn't throw a score. The Browns won, 15-7. Bradshaw was simply not taking his team into the end zone. He couldn't take it in from the five, the 10, or the 12, and that's losing football.

"I'm having trouble with my passing form," he said. "I'm just not setting up right and there's no zip on the ball. I haven't been throwing the way I did in college."

The next game was against Buffalo, and Pittsburgh finally won one, 23-10. Yet Terry was only three for 12 for 24 yards. Hanratty played a good part of the game and was instrumental in the victory. It began to look as if Noll would alternate his quarterbacks the rest of the way.

After four games, the man with the golden arm had completed just 33 passes in 83 attempts for a 39.8 percentage. He hadn't thrown for a single score and had been intercepted five times. In addition, he was dropped for a safety in each of the first three games. His performance on the heels of the fine exhbition season was a complete mystery.

The next week Terry tossed his first TD, a 67-yard bomb to Ron Shanklin and it gave Pittsburgh a 7-3 win over Houston. Then the word came out of the Steeler camp that the quarterback had been fined for missing a squad meeting. He had returned to Louisiana to visit his ailing mother and failed to make it back on time.

Then, two weeks later, the bottom fell out of Terry Bradshaw's season. He had been 12 for 27 for only 138 yards and four intercepts in a 31-14 loss to Oakland. Then, playing against Cincinnati, he couldn't do anything right, hitting just four of 12 for 40 yards. Noll yanked him early and Hanratty came on to lead the club to a 21-10 victory.

After the game, Terry lost his cool for the first time. Talking to reporters well within earshot of Hanratty, Terry said, "I don't want to play second fiddle to Terry Hanratty. I wouldn't mind if it was someone older, someone ready to retire, but I sure won't play behind someone my age. If the Steelers are planning on that, they better trade me."

The pop-off was ill-timed and even more ill-conceived. Noll was visibly upset and simply retorted by saying that "Terry has a lot of growing up to do, both on and off the field."

A Steeler player, who preferred to remain anonymous, told a Pittsburgh sports writer a few days later what the rest of the players thought of Bradshaw. "I think Terry lost the respect of some guys when he made the crack about being traded and rapped Hanratty. Heck, Hanratty never once griped when Noll played Bradshaw. He took it like a pro, and as a veteran, he probably had more reason to gripe than Bradshaw did."

Nothing worked well after that. Terry didn't even get into the game against the New York Jets the following week. Hanratty went all the way and the club won, 21-17. From that point on, with the exception of one other game, Hanratty was the starter with Bradshaw pitching relief. According to one story, Bradshaw's frustration grew so great that he went out to his car after one game and cried.

Seasoned observers could sense the team's on-field attitude changing. "The blocking appeared crisper, the holes a little wider when Hanratty ran the team," one said.

There were some incredibly bad days, like a three-for-20 afternoon against Green Bay and a three-for-12 outing against Atlanta. In the finale against Philadelphia, Terry didn't play long enough to throw a single pass.

Terry was a hero just once, in the second game with Cleveland. He completed just four of nine, but they were long ones, going for 197 yards and two TD's. The team won that one, 28-9. Otherwise, all the games were losses, and when it was over the Steeler record was 5-9, and that was after a 4-4 start.

The final statistics were appalling. Terry Bradshaw, the most talked about rookie since Namath, had completed just 83 of 218 passes for 1,410 yards. His passing percentage was an atrocious 38.1. He threw just six TD's, was intercepted 24 times and sacked 25 times. Hanratty didn't do much better with percentages. Yet his experience showed as he threw just eight intercepts and was sacked only three times. He had five TD passes.

If someone wanted to make a direct comparison with rookie Namath, Broadway Joe's 1965 stats read 164 completions in 340 attempts, a percentage of 47.2, with 2,220 yards gained, 18 touchdowns, and just 15 intercepts. It was quite a difference.

Asked about his season, Terry had to be honest. "I wouldn't want another year like it for anything in the world. But on the other hand, I got much of the experience I needed. I created a bad press with my mouth and bad performance with my arm.

"As the season went on I was losing confidence steadily. I just wasn't doing my job. When I was over, I just wanted to get away from Pittsburgh as fast as I could. I wanted to go home, stay away from football so I could relax and get the season out of my mind."

Fortunately, the young mind is capable of bouncing back. By February, Terry reported that he was mentally ready and anxious for the new season to start. "This time I'd have to beat out Hanratty on my own. If I didn't produce on the field, he'd play and well deserve it. I just had to be in the right frame of mind, despite the terrible letdown of my rookie year.

"To be honest, I thought I could do it all in one year, I really did. I didn't realize that in pro football you start from scratch. You have to relearn everything from the very beginning. It's a brand new ballgame all the way."

Terry did a lot of thinking during the off-season. Pretty soon, he began seeing stories in the newspapers, stories which were building up another quarterback, Jim Plunkett of Stanford, who would be entering his rookie year with the New England Patriots. The adjectives were all so similar to those used to describe Terry the year before. The stories had a familiar ring.

In May, a reporter asked Terry if he had any advice for young Plunkett, or for that matter, for any upcoming rookie quarterback.

"It'll be one of those years," said Terry, "in that they'll be great days and bad days. But the secret is to keep cool, not let the bad days eat at you for too long. That's the thing I didn't do last year.

"I wouldn't trade my rookie year for anything. But I really wouldn't want to ever go through that again. Of course, I would have been better off if I kept my mouth shut. That's part of keeping your cool. Then if you keep studying and keep learning, you'll be all right.

"There's just so much football to learn. That's the

important thing. If you throw an interception, forget it. If you have a bad game and they boo you, forget it."

As for the rest of his season, Terry had other regrets, like popping off about playing behind Hanratty and causing a split in the team. Yet he maintained that it was his basic determination that caused the ill-timed remarks.

"I'm not ashamed of the content of those remarks," Terry confessed. "I wouldn't want to play behind Bart Starr or Roman Gabriel, either. It just so happens that Hanratty's the guy here. My tone and timing may have been all wrong, but I meant what I said in that I don't intend to sit the bench. I plan on being the quarterback of the Steelers, the starting quarterback, and that's the only way I can look at it."

Once training camp opened at St. Vincent College in Latrobe, Pennsylvania, it was obvious that Terry was out to prove himself once more. His tremendous physical assets once again made him the man Pittsburgh seemed to be depending on. Forgetting the disciplinary incidents of the first year, Coach Noll went back to praising his handsome young signalcaller.

"He can stick the ball in there like nobody else," said Noll.

And John Fuqua, the Steelers top runner, indicated that the rest of the squad had forgotten the uneasiness of the previous season. All they were thinking about was football.

"A lot of things confused Terry last year," said Fuqua. "But now when you stand with him in the huddle at practice you can see there's a difference. He calls the defenses and is seeing more things, like where the linebackers are moving. He didn't notice these things at all last year."

Noll also pointed out an interesting statistic about

the club. "Our passing percentage as a team was just 38 percent last year, but our average gain per completion was the best in the league. So our quarterbacks were doing something right. We know we can strike for distance. Now we need greater consistency, especially in short-yardage situations."

In an exhibition game against arch-rival Cincinnati, Terry moved the club well, but still had trouble with the inconsistency. He got the only Steeler touchdown on a short run, but also got his bell rung in the fourth quarter, prompting a couple of Bengal defenders to say that he was running the ball too much. "If he keeps doing that, he'll really get hurt," said tackle Steve Chomyszak.

The Steelers finished the exhibition season with a 3-2 mark, but when the club opened the regular season against Chicago, it looked suspiciously like 1970 all over again. Bradshaw was named the starter after another fine preseason, but somehow he caught a case of the jitters again when it began for real.

He completed just 10 of 24 passes for 129 yards. He failed to throw for a touchdown and had four of his tosses picked off by an alert Chicago secondary. Still, it took two fumble recoveries in the last four minutes for the Bears to push across the scores that gave them a 17-15 victory.

After the game, Noll reaffirmed Bradshaw as his number one quarterback, claiming that Hanratty was strictly a backup performer. He also said that the news media buildup was hurting Terry's game. The only encouraging part of the Bear game was that the Steelers won the battle of statistics.

The next week against Cincinnati they won, 21-10, with Terry connecting on 18 of 30 passes for 249 yards. He hit Dave Smith with a 16-yard TD toss, then flipped a 13-yarder to Preston Pearson. When Terry came back with a 15-of-24 performance in a win over San Diego, it was beginning to look as if he was finally finding the touch.

He completed 12 of 27 against Cleveland, 20 of 39 versus Kansas City, 21 of 32 against Houston, and 20 of 35 when the Steelers met Baltimore. Bradshaw was much better, yet the club's record was 3-4. There were still a few holes to be filled, especially on defense, and it didn't appear as if the team would do much better than that. Yet some experts saw the potential and began counting the Steelers as one of the clubs with a bright future.

There were some inconsistencies in the second half of the year. In a big win over Cleveland, Terry completed just four of 11 for 70 yards, before being replaced by Hanratty. He came back to have a tremendous 25 of 36 day against the Dolphins, throwing for three scores before Miami pulled it out in the final seconds. But he was just six of 17 against Denver and 14 of 31 versus Houston. That prompted his only benching of the season. But he came off the bench to throw fourth-quarter touchdowns to Fuqua and Ron Shanklin in a 21-13 upset of the Bengals.

Coming into their final game, the Steelers were 6-7. They wanted a win, so that they would have a .500 season. But they'd be playing the powerful Los Angeles Rams, and it wouldn't be easy.

In the Cincinnati game, Hanratty fractured a collarbone. Noll had used rookie Bob Leahy before turning to Bradshaw that day. But when Terry pulled it out, he assured himself a start for the finale.

Terry admitted that he had lost some of his confidence in the second half of the 1971 season. Yet he knew where he wanted to go as a quarterback.

"I've got to learn to control the ball better," he said. "That's the first thing. Then I've got to cut down on the interceptions. And, finally, I've got to start coming up with the big play on more occasions. When I sit back and evaluate this season, I'll see how far I've come to attaining these goals. If I feel I've made progress, I'll be satisfied. I certainly wasn't satisfied with my first year."

There was one final disappointment. The Rams were simply too tough for the young Steelers. Los Angeles jumped to a quick 13-0 lead in the first quarter, and Terry had to play catch-up football. He tossed a three-yard TD pass to tight end Larry Brown in the second period, and a two-yarder to Shanklin in the third. But he also threw four more interceptions, and the Rams won, 23-14.

So another year had ended. The Steelers were 6-8, and Terry Bradshaw was still no superstar, though his 1971 season marked a vast improvement over 1970. He had thrown the ball 373 times, completing 203 for 2,259 yards. His passing percentage was up to 54.4. On the other hand, he threw for just 13 touchdowns as compared with 22 interceptions. He was the eighth-ranking passer in the AFC.

Terry gave much of the credit for his improvement to new quarterback coach Babe Parilli. "The man taught me so much," said Bradshaw. "He taught me things about football I didn't even know existed. He made me into a quarterback instead of just a thrower. I think the statistics speak for themselves."

Parilli gave the praise right back. "Joe Namath is a great quarterback," said the Kentucky Babe, who once played behind Broadway Joe. "And Terry Bradshaw is going to be a great quarterback. Joe can't set up to pass

any quicker than Terry. And his arm is as good as anyone's, anywhere. All he needs now is more experience.

"At the end of last season he was starting to realize
that he could gain as much yardage with a short pass,
rather than a long bomb. His receivers are the ones
who can cover the ground. But his playcalling improved and he got away from the hit-or-miss tendencies
of his rookie year."

The Steelers looked to be a much-improved club in
1972. The defense was quickly evolving into a crack
unit. Flanker Frank Lewis, a second-year man from
Grambling, and rookie fullback Franco Harris of Penn
State, were giving the team a big lift on offense. Kicker
Roy Gerela had one of the better toes in the league.
This time all the pressure wasn't on Terry.

Pittsburgh had a tough opponent in the opener, the
brutal Oakland Raiders, a team whose defense had
been chewing up quarterbacks for years. But this time
Terry Bradshaw was ready for them.

In the first quarter, Pitt linebacker Henry Davis gave
his club a big boost by blocking a punt, grabbing the
ball, and carrying it into the end zone. Minutes later,
another young linebacker, Jack Ham, intercepted an
Oakland pass. Terry moved the club to the Raider 21,
then bolted up the middle on a surprise keeper play
and blasted through the Oakland secondary all the way
to paydirt. It was a 14-0 game.

Oakland rallied for a score, then Bradshaw brought
his team into position for two Gerela field goals. Another march produced Terry's second TD as he scored
on a three-yard plunge. The score was 27-7. But then
the Raiders came back to score 21 fourth-quarter
points and take the lead, 28-27. It looked like the old
Steelers again.

Only this time Bradshaw kept his cool. With the ball

on his own 43, he dropped back, stayed in the pocket, and lofted a long pass in the direction of Ron Shanklin. The fleet receiver grabbed it near the goal line and went in untouched to complete the 57-yard play. The Raiders held on to win it, 34-28. Terry had completed just seven of 17 passes, but he hit when it counted, ran beautifully, and kept control of the game. For his efforts, he was named Associated Press Player of the Week.

Terry was modest, claiming he didn't deserve the honor, but it boosted his confidence nevertheless. He needed it. The next week the club was beaten by Cincinnati, 15-10. There were several questionable calls, however. Terry threw one TD pass to Shanklin that was called back, and connected with another long one that would have had the club knocking on the door. But the officials ruled that Shanklin was out of bounds when he caught it. Later, a Gerela field goal was blocked. The Steeler defense hadn't been bad. Cincinnati got all its points on five field goals by Horst Muhlmann.

Somehow, it wasn't a typical loss, and the club rebounded quickly to defeat St. Louis, 25-19. The next week, Dallas whipped Pittsburgh in another close one, 17-13, and suddenly the season had reached an early turning point. But there was another event that was to greatly alter the course of the year. Strangely enough, it had nothing to do with Terry Bradshaw.

In the Dallas game, fullback Preston Pearson sustained a serious injury, and rookie Franco Harris was installed in his place. The next week Pittsburgh beat Houston, 24-7, as Harris rambled for more than 100 yards. Three more big wins folllowed, against New England, Buffalo, and Cincinnati. In each game, the 6-2, 230-pound Harris ran wild, going over the century mark and evoking comparisons with the great Jim Brown. He gave the Steelers the big running game they'd always lacked, and helped take even more of the pressure off Terry.

The Steelers were 6-2 and in contention for the Central Division title in the AFC. And Steeler fans, who had focused on Terry for two years, were discovering other heroes—Harris for one. Franco had a black American father and an Italian mother. Suddenly, Italian-American fans of the Steelers formed "Franco's Italian Army," sat together with banners, and rooted for the big running back.

Another group of fans were taken by the sensational soccer-style kicks of Gerela, and they formed a rooting section called "Gerela's Gorillas." Not to be outdone, some Slovak fans rooted for "Dobre Shunka," the "Great Ham," in honor of linebacker Jack Ham who was having an all-pro season. The Steelers had an identity now, and with the pressure off, Terry could just go out and run the football team.

After beating Kansas City, the Steelers were upset by Cleveland, 26-24, to throw the divisional race into a two-team affair. A win over the Vikings seemed almost routine, as all the Steelers looked forward to the rematch with the Browns. The winner would likely take the title.

The game was played in Pittsburgh on December 3, and more than 55,000 fans came out to cheer their beloved team. The Steelers hadn't won in 40 years of NFL competition. Now the whole town was wild.

Cleveland took the opening kickoff. But four plays later Bo Scott fumbled and linebacker Andy Russell recovered it. Bradshaw came on, and moved the team to the 29. Then Gerela booted a perfect 36-yard field goal. Gerela's Gorillas went wild, as did the rest of the fans, and Pittsburgh was on the scoreboard at 3-0.

Harris ran for a touchdown early in the second quarter to make it a 10-0 game. Meanwhile, the Steeler defense was completely blanketing Mike Phipps and the Browns.

It stayed 10-0 into the third quarter. That's when Ham got into the act, intercepting a Phipps pass and running it to the Browns' six. After an exchange of fumbles, Harris scored his second touchdown and it was 17-0. A few minutes later, Terry reminded fans about his throwing arm, winging a 78-yard TD pass to Lewis. Gerela added another pair of field goals, and Pittsburgh won the ballgame, 30-0.

Two weeks later, the Steelers closed with a 24-2 victory over San Diego and had themselves an 11-3 season, a divisional title, and a trip to the NFL playoffs.

The year's sensational performances by so many of the Steeler players took Terry out of the limelight for the first time in his career. Franco Harris was great all year. He had gained 100 or more yards in six straight games and finished fourth in the AFC with 1,055 yards on just 188 carries. His 5.6 average per carry was among the best in the league. Fuqua complimented him with 665 yards on 150 carries. Gerela finished second to the Jets' Bobby Howfield in scoring with 119 points, making good on 28 of 41 field goal attempts.

As for Terry, he had a steady, albeit unspectacular season. But he was still the engineer of the 11-3 mark, and that couldn't be ignored. Statistically, he completed 147 of 308 passes for 1,887 yards and 12 touchdowns. He wasn't throwing as much because of the powerful running attack. His percentage was just 47.7, but he reduced his interceptions to 12, and that had to be a big plus.

With the newly effective zone defenses, many teams were throwing more to their tight ends, and that was a weak point in the Pittsburgh offense. Shanklin was the leading receiver with 38 catches. It wasn't yet an all-pro year for Bradshaw, but it was surely his most consistent since coming up.

"I think I've matured both on and off the field," he told reporters. "My biggest adjustment has been learning to read defenses, but I feel I've made good progress and will continue to make progress."

One Pittsburgh newsman who had covered the team since Bradshaw came had this to say. "Terry Bradshaw had a good season. The development of some of the club's younger players took the pressure off him and also took him out of the spotlight. That was good. He still hadn't proved himself a super quarterback, but he gave the team what it needed to win and once again showed his tremendous potential."

In the opening round of the playoffs, the Steelers had to face powerful Oakland. They remembered their opening-day 34-28 win against the Raiders, but so did the Raider players. Said fullback Marv Hubbard: "Nobody has beaten us twice in a row. Some teams in our division beat us, but when we played them again, we got even."

The game was played at Pittsburgh on December 23. It will go down as one of the best and strangest games in NFL annals. The two teams were similarly matched, with strong defenses on both sides. For the first half, it was just that, an epic defensive battle, neither team able to score. It began to look as if neither team would break the ice. Oakland's Daryle Lamonica wasn't throwing well, the Pittsburgh line contained their running game. Bradshaw was doing better, but his receiving corps was depleted by the loss of Lewis to an injury, so the Raider defense was keeping them honest.

Midway through the third period, Terry led a drive downfield that stalled at the 11. Gerela came on and booted an 18-yard field goal. The Steelers were on the scoreboard. In the fourth period, it happened again, this time Gerela hitting from the 29. It was 6-0, with the game entering the final session and the Pittsburgh fans beginning to taste victory.

Then Raider coach John Madden made a move. He installed young Ken Stabler at quarterback. Stabler began moving the team, and with about a minute and a half left, he had his club at the Pittsburgh 30. Stabler faded to pass, saw his receivers covered, and took off. Suddenly, he had a wall of blockers in front of him and he streaked down the sideline toward paydirt. The Steeler crowd couldn't believe it as the young QB ran into the end zone for a score. The kick by ancient George Blanda put the Raiders on top, 7-6, for the first time. There was just a minute and thirteen seconds left.

The kickoff went out of the end zone and the Steelers had it at the 20. Bradshaw had to move the team at least close enough for Gerela to have a shot at a three-pointer.

It was no secret that Terry would have to throw. That he did, dropping back five straight times. Two were broken up by free safety Jack Tatum, and two connected with receivers, bringing the ball to the 40-yard line of Pitt. There were five seconds left when Terry Bradshaw faded back to throw his final pass.

The original play called for Terry to throw at reserve wide receiver Barry Pearson. But Pearson was covered. Instead, Terry threw over the middle toward halfback John Fuqua. Fuqua was covered by one defender and Tatum rushed up to bat away the ball. It descended into the maze of bodies, then deflected backwards about seven yards. For a split second all action stopped. It looked as if the game was over.

Then there was movement. Franco Harris was streaking toward the Raider goal line with the football. One Oakland defender took up the chase, but it was too late. Harris rambled the remaining 40 or so yards to complete ... to complete what? For a minute, no one knew what had happened.

Gradually, it became clear. The football had deflected off Tatum's chest. Since Fuqua hadn't touched it, the ball was still in play. Harris, who was actually not involved in the original pattern, suddenly saw the pigskin coming at him. Instinctively, he grabbed it and took off. By the time the startled Raiders recovered, Harris had gone all the way in. The play was legal. The Steelers had won the ballgame, 13-7.

The play was viewed time and again on replay to erase any doubts about its legality. But the Steelers had won. Terry had completed 11 of 25 for 144 yards, but he was helped immensely by the final turnabout, and refused to take any credit for what happened. Now Pittsburgh would meet unbeaten Miami for the AFC crown. There was no time to rest on any laurels.

There was plenty of pre-game publicity during the week, focusing on the Dolphins' 15-game winning streak, and the powerful young Steelers. Then on Thursday, word came out of Pittsburgh that Terry Bradshaw was in the hospital, knocked out by a 24-hour virus, a strength-sapping ailment that can leave the victim weak and unsteady.

"I'll be ready by game time," Terry told the press. "You can bet on it. I'm just here to rest and get my strength back. One thing I've got is plenty of time to think about Miami."

Once more the Steelers had the home field advantage, and their fans swarmed all over Three Rivers Stadium. Terry was on the field looking no worse for wear and he started the game. Midway through the first period he had his club driving. With the ball at the three, Terry carried around left end. He was hit hard at the goal line and fumbled the ball, but tackle Gerry Mullins fell on it for a Steeler touchdown. It gave Pittsburgh a 7-0 lead, but Terry was shaken up on the play.

Still, Pittsburgh was dominating. Midway through the second period they held Miami again and Larry Seiple dropped back to punt at his own 38-yard line. He took the snap, started his motion—then suddenly took off and ran. The Steelers were caught napping and Seiple carried the ball 50 yards down to the Pittsburgh 12. It was a turning point. Two plays later Earl Morrall passed to Larry Csonka for the score.

On the Steeler side, there was another change. Bradshaw was still woozy from being hit at the goal line and Hanratty was running the team. He couldn't move it. Gerela booted a 14-yard field goal in the third period, but Miami came right back on a Griese-to-Warfield pass for 52 yards. A short run by Jim Kiick made the score 14-10 after three periods.

Steeler fans still believed in miracles. But the Dolphins were now controlling the game. They drove down again and scored, Kiick taking it in for a second time. With the score at 21-10, the Steelers were getting desperate. Chuck Noll put Terry Bradshaw back in the game.

Weakened by his illness and by getting racked up, Terry nevertheless went to work. He just started firing the football. Three completed passes brought it to the Miami 12, and a fourth to Al Young gave Pittsburgh a touchdown. It was 21-17, and it looked as if Bradshaw was hot.

But when the Steelers got the ball again, the magic was gone. The Dolphin defense was laying for Terry, and two of his final three passes were picked off and Miami won the ballgame.

Terry had played about half the game and completed five of 10 passes for 80 yards. It was a disappointing finish. Mean Joe Greene, the huge tackle, expressed Pittsburgh's sentiments when he said, "We still think we have the best team. They're good, but small mistakes made the difference."

No one put the rap on Bradshaw. He went as far as he could under adverse circumstances. He had been really racked on the goal line play, and having been sick so close to game time must have hurt. But he was now playing with a good young team, full of exciting talent.

"This is the team of the future, no doubt about it," Terry Bradshaw said during the 1972 season. "And it doesn't matter who's quarterbacking them."

But to the Steeler fans, players, and management, it does matter. If the Steelers are the team of the future, they still expect Terry Bradshaw to be the quarterback of the future. It hasn't been easy for him, jumping from Louisiana Tech to the Pittsburgh Steelers amid all that ballyhoo. But he's already realized his initial goal. He's helped make the team a winner.

And the way Terry and his teammates have been playing, a Super Bowl championship might not be far off.

FRAN TARKENTON

In 1967, a quarterback named Fran Tarkenton made a prophecy about the future:

"I think the quarterback of tomorrow is going to be better than we are today, and he will be able to do a zillion things, including scrambling. He's going to have the ability to throw from the roll, the moving pocket, the dropback pocket, the bootleg and the busted play. The quarterbacks coming out of the colleges nowadays are better athletes than ever before; they can do everything."

Although he himself may not admit it, Fran Tarkenton was the first of this new breed. The Landrys, Staubachs, Douglasses, Mannings, Plunketts, and Bradshaws have come on the scene to perform much as he prophesied.

Today's National Football League signal-caller is generally bigger, stronger, and faster than the men who came before him. And Fran Tarkenton as predicted, he can do more things.

The old-school quarterback was essentially a passer.

He would drop back seven or eight yards, set up behind a wall of protective blockers, pick out a receiver, and let fly. His arm was accurate and deadly.

But passing was his job. If he didn't throw, he'd hand the ball off to his backs, then get safely out of the way. Rarely, he'd take off and run. And when he did, everyone in the stadium would hold his breath hoping the passer wouldn't be hurt.

Now the game has changed. Defenses have become more sophisticated. The defenders are quicker, more highly specialized, and faster reacting. The quarterback has had to keep pace with everyone else. And the youngsters coming up today epitomize that change. They can still rifle the ball to a cutting receiver, but if trapped, they can run—and with authority. There is still the risk of injury. Roger Staubach got racked up that way and lost a season. But Bobby Douglass of the Bears ran for 968 yards in '72—better than most halfbacks ever do.

And the QB's not only throw from the pocket. Like Tarkenton, they can roll out, use a moving pocket, and scramble out of trouble waiting for a receiver to get clear.

When Fran first joined the Minnesota Vikings in 1961 as a rookie out of the University of Georgia, the ranking quarterbacks were Unitas, Tittle, and Jurgensen. His coach was Norm Van Brocklin, just a year in retirement. All four were classic throwers. Then along came Tark, winning the starting job his rookie year and astounding the football world with his helter-skelter style of play.

The Vikes were a brand new expansion team that year, glued together with a strange mixture of veterans, castoffs, and rookies. Yet Fran directed the team with the dash and daring of a veteran. With a weak offensive line unable to stop the opposition's pass rush, Fran had to run for his life. NFL veterans weren't used to chasing a cat-quick, fleet quarterback and his style mystified them. He was a winner in his first pro game and led his team to a pair of first-year victories after that.

By the time the season ended, he was being hailed as the best quarterback since . . . uh, Fran Tarkenton. After all, no one had seen anything quite like him before, and for want of a better description they began to call him a scrambler.

As the years went on, his style caused more than its share of controversy. There were pros and cons as to its ultimate effectiveness, but none of that induced Fran to alter his basic game. It's taken more than ten years, but Fran Tarkenton is at least receiving recognition as one of the finest quarterbacks in football. Statistically, he's among the top five all-time QB's and no quarterback has ever gained more yards rushing.

The frustrations of playing against Fran the Scram have been felt by many a pro lineman. Fran plays the game of now-you-see-me, now-you-don't, and a player had better be in shape to go up against him.

Hall-of-Famer Gino Marchetti, one of the finest defensive ends that ever played, couldn't believe what he'd go through against Tarkenton.

"We were going up against this young kid and I thought it would be easy," recalled Gino. "Then he started running around back there. I had him one time, I thought, I've really got him good. He was right in front of our bench with his back to me. I couldn't miss.

"So I really cut loose and what happens? He's going the other way and I'm tackling air. It was like he had eyes in the back of his head . . . unless he heard me huffing and puffing behind him."

And another all-pro lineman, former Green Bay

tackle Henry Jordan, once confessed to a recurring nightmare about Tark.

"I'd be chasing him all over the place," said Jordan, "trying to grab him—always trying, and always failing."

In reality, that was almost the way it was. Jordan described what it was like after an actual game with the Vikings in 1966. "The little son-of-a-gun would take off and I'd start chasing him. Suddenly the center would pop me from the blind side. I'd get up and start after him again. Another guy came from somewhere and decked me. All the while he was still scrambling around. Now I was determined to get him, but when I got up and started after him, someone blasted me again.

"When a guy like me has to run and cut and dodge around the backfield it can be dangerous. I'm always set up for a blind-side block. He just keeps you off balance and makes it pretty tough by running you hard play after play after play."

The testimony is endless. Fran is no fun to play against. But it certainly hasn't been all roses for the original scrambler. An exceptionally durable player who's never missed a pro game due to injury, Francis has had the misfortune of being in the wrong place at the wrong time as far as being on a winning team is concerned.

The Vikes were an expansion club when Fran came along and he quarterbacked them for six seasons, bringing them more victories than any other expansion team up to that time. But the honeymoon ended and he was traded to the New York Giants. When Fran arrived on the scene, the Giants were trying to rebuild a crumbled dynasty. The Scrambler gave them many exciting moments for five seasons, but the club just didn't have the material to go all the way. Once more the losers' tag was hung around Tarkenton's neck.

So there was another trade and Fran started the 1972 season right back where he began his pro career—in Minnesota. In Fran's absence, the Vikings had built a championship team under new coach Bud Grant. In fact, the Minnesota defense was one of the best and the team had a 35-7 record over a three-year span. But they couldn't win the big one—the Super Bowl.

Most observers blamed it on the offense, and the lack of a top-notch quarterback. So the trade was made and Tark returned to Minnesota, with more pressure on him than ever before. But we're getting ahead of ourselves. There's a lot more to the Fran Tarkenton story than this. It's time to go back and start from the beginning.

Francis Asbury Tarkenton was born in Richmond, Virginia, on February 3, 1940. His father was a Methodist minister and named his son after the first Methodist bishop in America, Francis Asbury.

The Reverend Dallas Tarkenton moved his family to Athens, Georgia, when Fran was just a young boy, and that's where he did most of his growing up. Brought up in a religious home, the youngster was modest, quiet, courteous, and friendly. He was a good kid, and before long, a good athlete.

Fran began playing football at about age eleven, when he joined the Athens YMCA team. Coach Cobern Kelley immediately installed the quick youngster at quarterback. So Fran's been calling the plays for a long time.

The quickness that was already helping him avoid charging linemen also helped young Fran become a budding shortstop star. He played both sports with equal skill and it's hard to say which one he liked better. Then fate took a hand. Fran tried a throw from deep short one day and his baseball career came to an abrupt halt.

"I heard something go 'pop' in my elbow," Fran recalls. "That was it for baseball. I couldn't throw hard again. Yet it never bothered me when I threw the football. It must be because the two motions are different, and I guess I was lucky in that respect."

Three years later he joined the Athens High football team and a year after that was spearheading that club to the Georgia state championship. Fran was no slouch then, either. He held the number-one QB spot on a high-school team considered by many as one of the finest in a long while. When his high-school career ended, he'd won 14 letters, competing in all the major sports. But he showed the most proficiency when he was on the gridiron.

One of those who saw Fran and immediately took a liking to him was Wally Butts, coach of the University of Georgia Bulldogs. Butts first saw Fran when the scrambler was a junior at Athens High. Two years later he had Tarkenton pulling on a Georgia uniform and leading the Bullpup Frosh to an undefeated, untied season. Tark was already a shade over six feet tall and weighed about 175 pounds. He was quick, smart, and a fine ballhandler. Though his passing arm wasn't really strong, he had good accuracy and knew when to throw the ball.

When the 1958 season rolled around, sophomore Tarkenton found himself quarterbacking the number-two offensive unit. In the Bulldogs' opening game, Fran was on the bench watching Texas take a 7-0 lead into the third quarter. With the ball on the Georgia five-yard line, Coach Butts sent Francis into the game to shake things up.

That he did. The Longhorn defenders found themselves facing a sharp, confident quarterback. Mixing slick handoffs with short passes, Fran led the Bulldogs upfield, collecting one first down after another. With the ball inside the ten, Fran stepped back and calmly hit end Jimmy Vickers with the first touchdown pass of his college career. A play later he was passing successfully again, this time to Aaron Box for a two-point conversion that put Georgia ahead, 8-7.

The fact that Texas came back to win the game is almost irrelevant, for the incident shows the strong character of young Francis Tarkenton. He was so anxious to get into that first game that he kept bugging Coach Butts on the sideline until the coach put him in.

Francis saw spot duty the remainder of the season, completing just 16 of 30 passes for 175 yards. But he was a clutch performer even then: five of those 16 passes went into the end zone for touchdowns. And although he wasn't known as a scrambler in those days, he went for good yardage when he carried the football and played a sturdy game at defensive safety when used there.

By the time he returned for his junior year in 1959, Francis was ready to take command of the Bulldog offense. But there was a senior quarterback ahead of him with the number-one unit. Instead of grousing and brooding, Fran went to work with the second team, and before long had molded them into a crackling, sharp attack squad.

In those days there was no free substitution, and college coaches generally worked by whole units. At Louisiana State University, Coach Paul Dietzel had popularized three-platoon football, having a "white team," the first unit that played both offense and defense, and "go team" that specialized in offense, and the "Chinese Bandits," a defensive team that was sent in to stop enemy thrusts. That way, each unit had its own identity and sense of pride in its performance.

There was a similar setup at Georgia in 1959, and Tarkenton's unit became the offensive stars. In fact, so strong was their identity and effectiveness, that they soon became known as "Tarkenton's Raiders" and "Tarkenton's Music-Makers," and Georgia fans as well as Coach Butts began counting on them to put the points on the scoreboard in crucial situations.

Before long, Tarkenton had his Raiders moving, and the Bulldogs began mowing down Southeastern Conference opponents at an impressive clip. He completed six of seven passes in his first outing against Alabama. The next week he duplicated the feat, passing for 119 yards and a touchdown in a victory over Vanderbilt.

Opening it up even more against South Carolina, Fran passed for 127 yards and a score, hitting on 14 of 19 attempts and moving his Raiders downfield time and again with relative ease. By then, the plaudits were starting to roll in.

Asked about his junior star, Coach Butts said, "Francis is the most effective medium-range passer I've seen in the entire Conference. Plus he's developed into a real dangerous runner. He's always been a great ball-handler and play-caller all along."

Georgia was still unbeaten and leading the SEC when the team met tough Auburn in the second-to-last game of the season. It was a tooth-and-nail struggle all the way. With just 30 seconds left in the game, Auburn led, 13-7. Georgia had the ball on the Auburn 13-yard line with a fourth-down play coming up.

Fran stepped calmly into the huddle and set up what

might be his final play. He flooded the right side of the offense with pass receivers, bent over the center, and called signals. The Auburn defense shifted to the left to cover the ends.

At the snap he started rolling right, as if to go to one of his receivers streaking for the end zone. But it was a fake. Fran stopped suddenly, whirled to his left, and fired a strike to left end Bill Herron who was wide open for the score. Kicker Durward Pennington split the uprights with the point-after-touchdown and Georgia had won the game and the SEC crown.

The next week he completed 11 of 18 passes for 115 yards against Georgia Tech and the SEC champion Bulldogs accepted an invitation to face Missouri in the Orange Bowl game on New Year's day.

With the regular season over, league officials announced that Fran's 62 completions in 102 attempts had set a new conference mark with a 60.8 percentage. He was also named to the AP and UPI all-SEC offensive unit. But he wasn't through yet. He still had the Orange Bowl left, and with his flair for the dramatic, had saved his best for last.

The Georgia defense was up for Missouri that New Year's Day in 1960. And a capacity crowd at the Orange Bowl in Miami watched them stop one drive after another. Coach Dan Devine's Missiourians couldn't crack through. And when the Bulldogs went on offense, all eyes were on Francis Asbury Tarkenton.

Running the offense with his usual crisp play-calling and ball-handling, Fran had the Bulldogs moving. Only an inspired Missouri defense prevented him from running up a big score. But on two long drives, one of 62 and the other of 71 yards, he was practically unstoppable, capping each with long, exciting, scoring plays.

On the first he had the ball on the Missouri 29. He

took the snap, rolled to his left, then reversed his field, eluding two defenders before spotting right halfback Bill McKenny streaking down the sideline. Throwing on the run, Fran hit McKenny with a perfect pass, good for a 29-yard score. That made it 7-0.

The second march was just as exciting. Bringing the ball to the Missouri 33 on a series of running plays and several short passes, Fran then decided he was ready for the big one. This time he dropped straight back, saw his end, Aaron Box, cutting toward the goal line, and he fired. The pass settled in the receiver's arms just as he rambled into the end zone for a 33-yard TD toss. The kick made it 14-0, and that's the way it ended.

When it was over, Fran had completed nine of 16 passes for 128 yards and two scores, and had firmly established himself as one of the more outstanding quarterbacks in the country. Georgia backfield coach, Charley Trippi, himself one of the Bulldogs' all-time great tailbacks, praised young Francis endlessly. Said Trippi:

"Fran Tarkenton has a sixth sense of being able to locate an open receiver, and that's why he has such a high percentage of completions. He doesn't throw unless a man is open. And unlike most quarterbacks, he's at his best when he's rolling out or dancing around, faking one way or the other and waiting until he sees an open receiver. I predict a very successful pro career for him."

A foreshadowing of the scrambler that was to come. But Fran still had another year at Georgia. When he returned for his last season he was undoubtedly first string. Although the team had lost many fine players through graduation and had untried sophs at many key positions, Fran still provided plenty of excitement for SEC football fans.

Passing more than ever, he showed his all-around ability to run a team, averaging some 50 minutes a game on the gridiron, much of that at defensive safety, where the Bulldogs were weak. He completed 15 of 31 passes in the opener against Alabama, good for 152 yards and a touchdown. He was off and winging, and he didn't stop until there were no more games left to play.

One of the highlights of his season came in the game against Mississippi State. State took a 17-7 lead into the locker room at halftime and appeared to have the game locked up. But they didn't count on the lightning that was Fran Tarkenton.

Georgia started from its own 19 after the kickoff, and Francis went to work. He began directing a powerful drive, sticking pretty much on the ground, faking the pass and running it himself on rollouts and bootleg plays. Or he'd drop back, then slam the ball into the belly of his fullback on the draw play. He threw the ball just twice as he took his club all the way to paydirt. The ensuing kick made it 17-14.

The next time he got the ball, the Mississippi defense had made some adjustments to contain the Bulldog running game. Fran was ready for it. He completed six straight passes to bring the ball into field goal range and the tying boot.

Then with just three minutes left, Fran got the ball again and completed five more clutch passes, each to a different receiver, and set up the winning field goal, kicked in the final eight seconds of the game. In all, he completed an amazing 19 of 24 passes for 224 yards, his best throwing day as a collegian.

"Tarkenton gets his team a touchdown as fast as any quarterback I've ever seen," said Florida coach Ray

Graves. "He's the golden thread that weaves a pattern down the field to score."

When Georgia went up against Graves' Florida team, the coach was equally impressed.

"Tarkenton was not at his very best for Florida, having suffered an asthma attack the night before," he said. "But he showed us how fast he can get a touchdown. We were leading 22-0 at the beginning of the fourth quarter. Suddenly Fran completed three passes in four plays and brought the ball to our four. Then he faked a pass and ran it over himself. Within four minutes he led another drive right into our end zone and made it 22-14. By then he had a bad hip and couldn't go at full speed, but he was still moving the ball. He got it back with a little over a minute left and had it at our 31 and driving when the gun sounded. Another minute and he might have scored again."

Against Tulsa, Fran came out smoking. He went to the air and completed nine of 12 passes for 136 yards and two scores. Georgia was ahead, 38-9, at the half, and Mr. Tarkenton got the rest of the day off.

In games against Vanderbilt and Kentucky, Fran was rushed in on defense and made clutch interceptions in each contest to prevent almost certain scores. So he could catch the ball as well as throw it.

After the Tulsa game, that school's athletic director, Glenn Dobbs, another former all-America player, said: "Tarkenton is the best college quarterback I've seen in about four years, better even than Don Meredith of SMU. Meredith was a colorful player, but not the all-around star Tarkenton is."

And Gil Brandt, a scout for the newly-formed Dallas Cowboys of the NFL, said this about fleet Francis. "Tarkenton is the best T-quarterback I've seen this year. Right now we rate him number one, Northwestern's Dick Thornton number two, and Wake Forest's Norman Snead number three."

As for Wally Butts, Fran's coach, he didn't have enough to say. "We've had two all-America quarterbacks at Georgia, Johnny Rauch and Zeke Bratkowski, but I'd rate Francis a better all-around performer than either of them. He has no superior as a field general and ballhandler, and he's at his best in clutch situations."

There wasn't much more that could be said. Fran was doing it all and attracting plenty of attention. When the year ended, he was generally rated among the best college players in the land. He was a second team all-America on the Associated Press team behind Mississippi's Jake Gibbs. Once again he led the SEC in passing with 108 of 185 for 1,189 yards and seven touchdowns, good for a passing percentage of 58.4. He also led the conference in total offense with 1,274 yards, so it was obvious that he didn't run the ball very much.

In addition to all of that, it was an intelligent Tarkenton who graduated from the University of Georgia. He was a first team selection on the all-America Academic Squad, comprised of the best student-athletes in the land. He majored in Business Administration, burning the books as well as he burned up the gridiron. He had also found time to fall in love with one of the Georgia cheerleaders. Fran and Elaine Tarkenton became man and wife before graduation.

Georgia didn't do well enough to rate a bowl bid in 1960, but that didn't prevent Fran from participating in the annual Hula Bowl game in Honolulu after the season. Playing almost the entire game at quarterback, the elusive Tarkenton completed 19 of 33 passes for 204 yards and two touchdowns. They were the only scores at his East team whipped the West all-stars, 14-7. For his efforts Fran was awarded the Governor's Cup as the game's outstanding back, and the pro scouts began taking more notice than ever.

With his sound academic background, Francis could have jumped right into the business world and been successful. But the lure of the gridiron was great and he anxiously awaited the annual pro draft.

The year that Tark was up for the draft (1960) marked the first time there was open warfare between the older, established National Football League and the newly formed American League. Each league held a draft, then began bidding for the players. The AFL knew that to survive it would have to begin signing name players, and the league was offering huge sums of money to youngsters coming out of the colleges. Sometimes the NFL matched the offer, sometimes not.

In Fran's case, there was a good amount of competition involved. First he learned that he was the top pick of the Boston Patriots of the American Football League. Then he sat tight to hear how he fared with the NFL.

"It shook me up a little when I finally heard from the NFL," Fran recalls. "Bert Rose, the Vikings' general manager, called me and said his club was about to pick me as their third round draft choice. I could understand why they hadn't picked me earlier. After all, they had a veteran quarterback in George Shaw and as an expansion team they needed to shore up at other positions.

"But as far as I was concerned, good quarterbacks are usually picked first and I had a pretty good record at Georgia. I began to feel that if none of the clubs in the NFL thought enough of me to pick me first or second that I might be better off going to the American League."

The wheels started turning and sure enough the Patriots came in with the big offer, substantially above the figure mentioned by the Vikings. Fran was on the brink of taking it, but something kept him from agreeing. Finally, he knew what it was.

"I realized that I had to find out if I could play with the best," he said. "And that meant the National Football League. So I signed with the Vikings."

The Vikes hadn't picked Tarkenton out of the blue. Team management was well aware of the perils of an expansion club. A good offensive line can't be patched together overnight, and the team's quarterback would in all likelihood have to be a nimble-footed youngster who could run for his life if necessary, and chances were it would be often. They knew about Tarkenton's speed and quickness, plus he had a pretty good passing arm, so that was it.

Coach Norm Van Brocklin may not have been overwhelmed by the selection. Van Brocklin had ended a great career with a championship at Philadelphia the year before and stepped right across the line into coaching. Chances are Norm felt he could still be his own best quarterback, but he'd stick by his decision to quit. An expansion team was no place for an aging signalcaller, especially one cut from Van Brocklin's mold.

He was a classic passer, one of the best, and he did it the classic way, dropping back into the pocket and firing. He rarely ran with the ball. That wasn't his job. It was obvious that as a coach he'd eventually expect his quarterback to operate much in the same way. Yet he, too, knew that Fran Tarkenton had what the Vikings needed to begin.

When Van first met Tark he immediately suggested a program to build up the rookie's throwing arm.

"It isn't really anything too difficult," Fran explained. "The coach just has me pushing up a five-pound weight a few times a day before practice. I haven't been at it long and still don't see any results, but I'm sure it'll help me."

As for Van, he was satisfied with the youngster's early progress once training camp began.

"We got ourselves a good break with Fran when the All-Star squad didn't take him," said Van. "They got Tommy Mason and Rip Hawkins, and that hurt since we're counting on them as starters at halfback and middle linebacker. But we've got Fran here and can move ahead step by step working him into our attack. He may be useful to us before the season is over."

Van Brocklin was referring to the annual College All-Star game which pits the top collegians against the NFL champs. The fact that they didn't choose Tark was another indication that he wasn't regarded as a real pro prospect.

The man expected to start at quarterback for the Vikings was George Shaw, a player who always seemed to have the potential, but was never able to hold onto a number-one job. The thinking was that Shaw could do an adequate job in the QB spot until the team could develop Tarkenton or some other youngster.

But even before the first exhibition game started, Fran Tarkenton was showing signs of being more than just an ordinary rookie. One Minnesota scribe said it this way.

"It's still too early to evaluate Tarkenton as a passer, long or short. But he's already shown certain prerequisites for being a professional quarterback. He's dead sure of himself and reflects his own opinion that he has a perfect right to order people around, which is one thing a professional quarterback must do."

The rest, Van Brocklin himself was taking care of.

Being an ex-quarterback, the Dutchman, as he was called, worked with the youngster tirelessly. As night fell at the Vikes' training camp, the deserted practice field would have three solitary figures left. One was young Tarkenton, the other Van Brocklin, and the third one of the team's pass receivers recruited to help out.

Tarkenton would stand with the sweat pouring down his face, breathing heavily.

"Tired, Francis?" Van Brocklin would say.

Fran would manage a quick smile, take a deep breath, and go back to his routine. Under Van Brocklin's keen eye he'd give himself a signal, slap the football to simulate the snap from center, then drop back, weave, pump his arm and throw. They'd repeat the routine until Fran felt as if his arm was ready to fall off. When they finally quit, Van Brocklin would drape his arm around the youngster's shoulder and say,

"You're starting to get the idea. Just keep at it."

Fran did. In the first five days of real practice he showed that he had guts, taking the veterans' best shots and bouncing back for more. Van Brocklin had warned him that he couldn't let himself be intimidated by his opponents' rush. Otherwise, he'd lose the confidence of his own teammates. But it wasn't necessary to tell that to the youngster. No one was about to intimidate Fran.

Finally the first exhibition game rolled around. Shaw started against the Rams, but Fran knew he'd see action and he was ready. When he entered the game the Vikings were down, 21-3. He assumed control of the offense and suddenly it was like being at Georgia again. He moved the club with confidence and authority, and they seemed to respond under his leadership.

Quickly, the Vikes were in scoring position. Then Fran tossed a pass to end Dick Haley for a touchdown. Minutes later he had the club inside the 10 again. This time he carried it in himself on a bootleg play. The third time he drove the team down, he saw a 37-yard TD toss to rookie Mason nullified by a penalty. When it ended, the Rams had won, 21-17, but the young Vikings had really given them a scare.

"Is Tarkenton going to be your number one quarterback?" a reporter asked Van Brocklin after the game.

"I can't answer that now," said the diplomatic Dutchman. "I don't even know who my 42 players will be."

But a few minutes later the coach was talking to someone else and he casually remarked, "Maybe we've found the thing we need most—someone who can move the club." And there was little doubt about whom he meant.

On September 17, 1961, some 32,236 fans journeyed to Metropolitan Stadium to watch the NFL's newest entry play against their first game ever. It wouldn't be easy. The Vikings were up against the Chicago Bears, a rough-and-tumble squad ready to give the inexperienced Vikes a real baptism into the world of NFL football.

Van Brocklin started the veteran Shaw at quarterback and the Bears jumped out to a quick lead. The Minnesota offense looked sluggish and inept, and as predicted, the Bears were handling them with relative ease.

When the second quarter began, Van Brocklin was getting restless. Finally, he turned to his young rookie and said,

"Francis, get in there and get something going. Those guys need someone to wake them up."

Number 10 pulled on his helmet and trotted onto the field, much to the surprise of the Viking offense and big crowd. But it didn't take Fran long to do his job.

Soon after he checked in, he showed his club who was boss. Coming back to the huddle after carrying the ball, veteran halfback Hugh McElhenny started groaning: "Man, I'm tired."

Without batting an eyelash, Fran called McElhenny on the very next play, then ran his veteran back again on the play after that. Needless to say, Mac never complained about being tired again, at least not when Tark was in the game.

But that wasn't all Fran did. Before the half was over he had found McElhenny free in the end zone and hit him with a scoring pass. It put the Vikes right back in the ballgame. At the half, the mean Bears plotted to get the kid off their backs. They'd slam him into submission.

But you can't hit what you can't find. In the third period, Tarkenton began leaving the pocket to escape the Chicago rush . . . and he kept firing strikes. Three more times he found his veteran receivers open in the end zone, hitting first Jerry Reichow, then Dave Middleton, and finally Bob Schnelker for Viking touchdowns.

The Bears couldn't cope with the 190-pound lightning bolt that had hit them so unexpectedly. Once the defense yielded to Tarkenton's magic, the Chicago offense grew desperate and sloppy. They couldn't move, not even against the mediocre Minnesota defense. The impossible was happening, and the brand new Viking fans loved every minute of it.

When the final gun sounded they swarmed on the field, everyone trying to get their hands on the young quarterback. For Fran Tarkenton had led the expansionist Vikings to a shocking 37-13 victory over one of the NFL's better teams.

He did it by playing three quarters of flawless football, completing 17 of 23 passes for 250 yards and four touchdowns. In the third quarter alone he had connected on eight of 11 attempts to completely demoralize the Bears. After one week of play, the rookie was leading the entire National Football League in passing.

"The guy's a natural leader. I never saw anything like it," said the veteran McElhenny. "He just took charge and really let us know he was the boss out there."

McElhenny wasn't the only one praising Tarkenton. Rookies traditionally take a beating out there, especially in their first few games, yet Fran's performance was generally viewed as the greatest debut any rookie quarterback ever had. One newsman covering the Vikings revealed another interesting aspect of Tark's play.

"Fran Tarkenton performed with the poise of a 10-year veteran on Sunday," he wrote. "But it didn't surprise some people who have been watching the youngster's progress all summer. Tark didn't throw a single interception against the Bears. That, too, came as no surprise. You may find it hard to believe, but counting the exhibition season, this amazing rookie from Georgia hasn't had one picked off in 81 consecutive passing attempts. And how's that for poise?"

It was true. Fran's arm wasn't the most powerful in the league, but he was showing amazing accuracy, especially for a first-year player. One of the hardest things for a rookie quarterback to do is pick out his receivers. So many things happen on every play that the rookie often panics and throws into a crowd. Thus intercepts are usually frequent. But Francis was proving the exception, rather than the rule.

Still, an expansion club can only do so much. There are too many weak spots to hope for any miracles. The next week things changed. Minnesota played the one-year-old Dallas Cowboys, a winless expansion club the year before, and were soundly beaten, 21-7. They found their offense the week after that, but Baltimore squeezed past the Vikes, 34-33. Then Dallas shut them out, 28-0, San Francisco toppled them, 38-24, and Green Bay whipped them twice. A loss to Los Angeles made it seven in a row before Tarkenton engineered a 28-20 upset of the Colts for the Vikes' second win.

Two more defeats followed before the Rams came into Bloomington for their second encounter with the Vikings. By now, the Los Angeles team, as well as the rest of the league, were very much aware of the abilities of Fran Tarkenton. Despite the team's erratic showing, Francis was having an exceptional rookie year. He was completing more than 55 percent of his passes and had thrown for more than a dozen touchdowns. Any time he stepped onto the field he threatened to put points on the scoreboard.

Sure, he'd had some bad games, but many thought that was because of the men around him. In fact, some said the rookie from Georgia hadn't really played a bad game all year. He simply continued to do things that rookie quarterbacks were supposed to do.

Against the Rams, Tark was on top of his game. He was all over the backfield, dodging tacklers, sprinting away from pursuers, and driving the LA defenders to distraction. And he was throwing the ball like an all-pro. Four times he connected with his receivers in the Los Angeles end zone. When the smoke cleared, Francis had burned the Rams, 42-21, for his club's third victory, the most by any first-year expansion team to date.

Two final losses followed, though the Scrambler did put 35 points on the board against the Bears in the finale, only this time the Chicagoans scored 52 against a

Viking defense that showed little improvement over the course of the campaign. But none of that dimmed the rookie achievement of Francis Tarkenton.

Through 14 rugged games, Fran had completed 157 of 280 passes, good for 1,997 yards and a 56.2 completion percentage. His touchdown total of 18 was then the second-best mark for a rookie in NFL history. He was intercepted 17 times. As a scrambler, he was credited with 56 rushes for 308 yards and an average of 5.5 a carry. Tark's 56.1 passing percentage was also better than any previous NFL rookie. And he did it throwing under the most trying of football conditions—with a very weak offensive line.

By way of comparison, the great John Unitas completed just 110 of 198 as a rookie, good for 1,498 yards, a 55.6 percentage, and just nine touchdowns. Fran was already ranking up there with the best of them and he was drawing praise for it.

Norm Van Brocklin couldn't say enough about Tark after that first year. "Fran's got to be the best rookie quarterback to come into this league since Unitas," claimed the Dutchman. "His eagerness and ability to learn have impressed me from the start. I'd have to say that he's learned more in one year than most young signalcallers do in the first five or six years in the NFL.

"Right now I'd say that Fran Tarkenton is the most important man in the entire Viking organization."

And Van Brocklin wasn't alone. Veteran Hugh McElhenny called Fran "a natural leader, and the best rookie I ever saw."

Ram coach Bob Waterfield, once a great passing quarterback himself and a teammate of Van Brocklin's when the Dutchman came up with the Rams, had this to say: "Tarkenton shows unusual promise at quarterback. He scrambles around out there a lot, but once he learns to stay in the pocket, he'll be quite a quarterback."

While Waterfield's comment was undoubtedly intended to praise, it showed that many NFL people still thought of the quarterback as a classic drop-back passer. Although Fran's scrambling tactics were effective, many still doubted that they would be effective over a long period of time.

Early in the 1962 exhibition season, Fran led the Vikes to a 24-13 conquest of the Colts. That was the game in which Baltimore veteran end Gino Marchetti fully realized the frustrations of chasing a scrambler. And in that same contest, John Unitas called Fran a "real money player—best when it's toughest in there."

But once the season started, the still-inexperienced Vikings promptly dropped five straight, scoring just 21 points in their first four games. Suddenly, Tark found himself under the gun. He wasn't putting points on the scoreboard the same way he had the season before.

In game five, however, he had one of his patented offensive explosions, bringing the Vikes from a 34-7 deficit against Green Bay to 34-21 in a matter of minutes. The Pack went on to win, 48-21, and after the game an interesting story appeared in one of the Minneapolis papers.

It said that Coach Van Brocklin was attempting to "redesign" Fran Tarkenton, and that he was sacrificing wins to "develop the solid quarterbacking required on an NFL contender." It further said that Fran was allowed to scramble around as a rookie because it was Minnesota's only chance to win a few in its first season. And now that Van Brocklin showed the fans he could win with "a bunch of stiffs," he was seriously building toward the middle 1960's when he figured the Vikes would emerge as a legitimate contender.

And for the first time came the word that someone felt scramblers "can only achieve upsets, not championships." Against the Packers, Fran had completed 20 of 29 passes, many of them coming from the pocket, and not on scrambles.

A month later Van Brocklin was once again giving Fran a total vote of confidence, saying, "The quarterback is the heart of your team and we've got the best young quarterback in football."

Fran was on another of his scoring tears, leading the Vikes past the Rams, 38-31, and Eagles, 31-21. The following week he put another 31 points on the board as Minnesota lost to Pittsburgh by eight. Then, in a big game against the Bears, Francis had the Vikings on top, 30-28, with just 30 seconds to play. Bill Butler had intercepted a Bill Wade pass on the Minnesota 20, and all Fran had to do was run out the clock.

The easiest way to do that would be for Fran to take the snap and fall down. But instead, he handed off to fullback Doug Mayberry who promptly fumbled. The Bears recovered and Roger LeClerc booted a game-winning field goal with just 17 seconds remaining.

A dejected Fran admitted to making a bush mistake. "I don't even know why I handed off," he said. "Maybe I learned a lesson. I wouldn't do it again in that kind of situation. I'd just take the ball and fall down."

After that, the season was all downhill. The team lost four of its last five games and finished out at 2-11-1, scoring fewer points and giving up even more than the season before. Fran threw 22 more TD passes, but this time had 25 intercepted and compiled a passing percentage of less than 50 percent (49.5). Many football people blamed it on the scrambling, although

Fran's 361 yards on just 41 scrambles was impressive. He had gained 8.8 yards everytime he carried the ball.

But performances are gauged on victories, not individual statistics, and it was a lost year as far as Fran was concerned. He didn't feel that he showed enough improvement from his rookie season. Even the fans began to get on him during a season he later described as "miserable."

Said Fran, "I remember one game when I just wasn't playing well. I could hear some of the fans getting restless and a sort of low undercurrent of boos began spreading through the stadium. For the first time in my entire football career I began picking up things like, 'Get him out of there!' and 'We want McCormick!' John McCormick was my backup that year, and pretty soon Van Brocklin pulled me out and sent him in.

"It was sure a lonesome walk to the sidelines, listening to thousands of fans cheering my replacement. It was the first time since I'd been playing football that I'd been taken out because I wasn't playing well. I remember going to the sideline and having old Hugh McElhenny come over to me. He just put his arm around me and said, 'Well, kid, you've arrived. You're now an official NFL quarterback. They booed you and you've been yanked. Welcome to the club!' It had to be the lowpoint of my career."

But in some ways that season was a maturing experience for Tark. He himself admitted it. "I was 22 years old and a fresh kid from Athens, Georgia. I didn't fully understand why the fans didn't all love me and what I was doing. I had to have some sense knocked into me."

By the time the next season rolled around, there were new young players coming into the Viking camp. And many of those names appearing in the Minnesota roster were names that would later make up the heart of the powerful Viking units of the later sixties. But as youngsters, players like Grady Alderman, Ed Sharockman, Roy Winston, Mick Tinglehoff, Fred Cox, Jim Marshall, and Bill Brown still had a lot to learn. Nevertheless, one man happy to see them appearing on the scene was Fran Tarkenton.

"Sure, there are a lot of new faces here this year," Fran said, "and I think the team's offense will be 100 percent better. I don't want to minimize the contributions our veterans have made. But in a lot of cases they were players who had lost their zest for the game. Now there's no one here who fits that description.

"I guess you could call the Viking teams of the past two seasons interim teams. The one that you'll see this year will be the club that plays here for a long time."

When someone mentioned that one of the new players would be Wisconsin quarterback and Rose Bowl hero Ron VanderKelen, Fran reactive positively.

"It's a healthy thing to have competition, and I'm not really worried about it. In professional sports, a man is paid to produce and he has to let his performance stand for itself. If you're not producing, they move in somebody who might. That's the law of the game and everyone must accept it.

"If VanderKelen develops fast enough so that he can help the team in his first season I'll be glad of it. A person would have to be pretty conceited to think he was the only one on the club who could do the job."

Conceited, no. Prideful, yes. Fran Tarkenton felt the job of quarterbacking the Vikings was his and didn't really expect anyone to take it from him. In fact, he was looking forward to a big season in '63.

The season opened on September 15, with the Vikes going against the 49ers at San Francisco. In that game, Fran and the young Minnesota club lived up to its pre-season billing with a strong, 24-20, triumph, including two late scoring drives engineered by Tark. For his efforts, Francis was given the game ball.

"We gave it (the ball) to Francis for his leadership," said linebacker Steve Stonebreaker. "He brought the team together and scored those two late touchdowns, and that, in turn, inspired the defensive team to hold when it had to."

As for VanBrocklin, nothing made him happier than a win. "I don't think I've ever seen Fran better," said the Dutchman. "Naturally, I'm proud of him. I'm his coach."

But the basic pattern of the season was the same. The only difference was that the Vikings did everything a little bit better than before. They finished at 5-8-1, and seeing that the club was just three years old, everyone was pretty much satisfied that progress was being made and they were ready to turn the corner. More young players were coming and Fran Tarkenton seemed to be arriving.

He himself admitted, "I was still immature in 1963. It wasn't until the 1964 season that I began to feel like a genuine, bona fide professional quarterback, able to react properly to the pressure of the game.

Fran completed more than 57 percent of his tosses in 1963, and was named the Vikings' Most Valuable Player for the second successive year. And that same season the team produced its first all-pro player in halfback Tommy Mason. The college draft produced another blue chip defender in Carl Eller of Minnesota, so the team seemed to be coming right on schedule.

The 1964 season was significant for several reasons. It was the first in which the Vikings finished over the .500 mark, but it also marked the first time Van

Brocklin clashed openly with Fran over the quarterback's scrambling style.

For the first six games the Vikes played about as usual, having good days, then bad days, with the highlight being a 24-23 upset over the champion Packers. It was a typical Tarkenton coup. With one minute left, the Vikings trailed by two, 23-21. They had the ball with a fourth down and 22 yards to go, deep in their own territory.

Green Bay dropped its secondary back to prevent the long gainer, and ordered its linemen to blitz. Fran knew he wouldn't have time to throw ... that is, unless he scrambled. He faded back, saw no one open, and started to move.

First he eluded all-pro end Willie Davis with a quick sidestep. Then he moved to his right, back to his left, and the other way again before spotting tight end Gordy Smith downfield. Throwing on the run, Fran hit Smith for a 44-yard gain. With just 18 seconds left, Fred Cox came on and booted a 27-yard field goal to win it.

Some of the writers pointed out that only a scrambler could have completed that pass play. By leaving the pocket, Fran gave Gordy Smith the extra time needed to get free and gave himself time to throw. A conventional passer would have been buried by the brutal Packer pass rush.

Still, it was no secret that Van Brocklin wanted him to stay in the pocket except in dire emergencies. "When a quarterback takes off and runs," the Dutchman said, "he usually winds up in trouble. We'd like to see Fran step up and gun it ... in other words, to stay at home a little more." Van also said he thought Fran could release the ball faster if he just dropped back and fired, and that would make it easier on his receivers.

As for Francis, he felt compelled to defend his style, but he did it diplomatically. "Norm and I have worked together on my getting rid of the ball faster," he explained. "There certainly are times when I should have done it, but I also think there are times when I can help the club by scrambling for yardage if I don't see a receiver open."

The second half of the season was good. There were victories over San Fransisco, Los Angeles, the New York Giants, and Philadelphia, plus a hard-fought tie wth Detroit. The Vikes finished at 8-5-1 and in a tie with Green Bay for second place in the NFL's Western Conference behind Baltimore. Fran had completed 55.9 percent of his passes and struck for 22 touchdowns with only 11 intercepts. The club had scored 355 points, most in its history, but Van Brocklin wasn't satisfied.

"Fran just won't stay in the pocket," the exasperated coach said as the most-successful season neared its end. "I've tried time and again to get him to stay there, but even if I lock him up he finds a way to scramble around, looking for a receiver and trying to run away from a gang of tacklers.

"He's just as likely to go back 80 yards as he is to run ahead to 10. It's all right to have a running quarterback if you have three others to take his place. But no one has that luxury. I can't see risking any injury to a key player."

It was a strange statement in view of the fact that the scramblingest of all quarterbacks had never suffered a serious injury during his entire college and pro career. And despite Van Brocklin's steady stream of criticism, Fran had had a great season and he capped it by leading the West team to a 34-14 victory over the East in the annual Pro Bowl game. For his efforts he shared the game's outstanding player award with receiver Terry Barr.

Needless to say, big things were expected from the Vikings in 1965. Fran himself said he was looking forward to a 30-TD-pass season, and more top-notch players were joining the team. Running back Dave Osborn and defensive tackle Gary Larsen were to become regulars that first season. Some experts figured the Vikes to go all the way to the top spot in their division. But something happened. Let's let Fran himself tell about it.

"First of all we plowed through our exhibition season with five wins in five games," he recalls. "We crested in our next-to-last game with a 52-17 slaughter of Dallas. A few weeks later we were on our way to Baltimore for the opener and it was as if we were headed for the championship game right then and there. That's how high we were.

"Then we hit Baltimore and the temperature was 94 degrees. We'd been training in the cool north of Minnesota and it zapped us. I remember sitting on the bench between Bill Brown and Tommy Mason (both running backs) in the first quarter and they were breathing as though they had just picked an acre of cotton. Later our left guard almost passed out right on the field and had to leave the game. I had a bad day, too, and we lost, 35-16.

"The next week we were ahead of Detroit, 29-24, with 30 seconds left. Milt Plum, their quarterback, danced out of the pocket and connected with Amos Marsh on a 48-yard pass play, with Marsh making a circus grab of the ball to take it in. Suddenly our big year was plummeting at 0-2.

"But instead of folding we bounced back to beat the Rams and Giants. Just when it looked to be turning around, Gale Sayers beat us with a 96-yard kickoff returned in the closing minutes. Then we won three straight only to lose to Baltimore and Green Bay after that. I think that cooked us, because we then lost two more to San Francisco and the Packers again and we had to beat Detroit and Chicago in our last two to break even. So we finished the season on a very confused note with a record of 7-7. In our big year, the season in which we were supposed to win it all, we wound up fifth, a derelict of a football team."

During that terrible season of ups and downs the rumblings about Tark's style of play continued to build. Baltimore great John Unitas publically came out against scrambling, saying, "If you do a lot of running with those big guys chasing you, you'll eventually take too many knocks. Plus your receivers won't last as long, either, simply because they've got to scramble just to keep up with the passes.

"A roll-out quarterback can't possibly survey the whole field and pick out his best target because he's too concerned with his running and passing at the same time."

Tarkenton replied by saying that "a scramble is a reaction to a situation. I admit I can throw better standing still. When Unitas goes, it's called a run; with me, it's a scramble. The difference is that John runs on plan, while I run when I must. But I'll always go for the touchdown, even if I have to scramble."

But while people were calling Fran the game's most exciting quarterback, and enemy defenses were burning the midnight oil trying to figure how to contain him, Van Brocklin continued to lament.

"I just can't change him," the Dutchman told the press. "Scrambling is his style. When it gets to third and 40, I let him call the play."

There were no overly optimistic predictions about the 1966 season. It was apparent that the Vikings were still not a consistent club, and it was hard to see how they'd perform from week to week.

They opened with a 20-20 tie against San Francisco, then lost to Baltimore, Dallas, and Chicago before upsetting the Packers once more. But losses to Detroit, Los Angeles, and Green Bay followed and the club was finished with a 1-6-1 record in slightly more than half a season. It was a complete reversal of form and was the final, crushing blow between Fran, Van Brocklin, and the Viking management.

"We had our moments in '66," says Fran, "but they were widely spaced out. As the season wore on, I began to feel a great personal disenchantment. One by one, I was accumulating a full set of compelling, personal reasons of my own for leaving the team. And toward the end of the season I finally decided that this would be my last year with the Vikings. It was clear that my departure would be in the best interests of my teammates and myself."

The strange thing about it was that Van Brocklin was having the same thoughts. With just two weeks left in the season he told Fran and the rest of the Vikes that he was quitting. But within 24 hours the Dutchman had changed his mind. He had a long talk with Francis and the two made a tentative decision to try it again.

Fran went home to Atlanta after the season and in six weeks had made up his mind. He wrote a letter to Van Brocklin, sending copies to the team management, stating that he couldn't continue playing in Minnesota.

The letter said in part that "because of the events of the past few months and my feelings toward a number of things, it is impossible for me to return to the Vikings with a clear and open mind. . . ."

One day after the letter was received, Fran learned that Van Brocklin had quit again, this time for good. But it didn't alter Fran's thinking. He still wanted out.

It wasn't an easy decision for him. The things that were written and said in the next few months became an ordeal for him and his family. He never liked controversy and back-biting, and he claimed that the entire incident "tarnished the finest thing that ever happened to me in my life: my association with the Minnesota football players."

But he was his own man, had a clear mind, and felt he had done the right thing. He'd have to stick by his decision.

The jawing between Van and Fran continued. The Dutchman let it be known that during the 1964 season Philadelphia had offered Sonny Jurgensen to Minnesota for Fran, and while the assistant coaches voted 5-0 for the deal, Van Brocklin vetoed it. Then late in the 1966 season Van benched Fran in favor of young Bob Berry during a game that was being televised to Fran's home country of Atlanta. Tarkenton took that as a further slap in the face. So many things had happened that could no longer be ignored.

Early in 1967 a rumor began to spread around Yankee Stadium in the Bronx. It was simple. The word was out that the Giants were going to swing a deal for Fran Tarkenton. New York fans swooned. Their beloved Giants, once an NFL power, had just completed a 1-12-1 season in '66. Naturally, the team had many deficiencies, but one of the biggest was at quarterback, a position that hadn't been filled since Y. A. Tittle retired a couple of years earlier.

In addition, the Giants' crosstown rivals, the New

York Jets, were being run by a QB named Joe Namath, and the flamboyant Broadway Joe had taken the town by storm. The exciting, scrambling Tarkenton was needed desperately to put some more punch and glamour in New York Giants football.

The trade was completed in early March of 1967. To get Tarkenton, the Giants gave up their first and second draft choices for 1967 to Minnesota, plus their first pick in 1968. Some people said the price was too high, but Giants coach Allie Sherman disagreed.

"You have to give up a lot to get a lot," said Allie. "We needed a top quarterback and that's just what Fran Tarkenton is. We had the opportunity to get one of the best quality quarterbacks in the NFL. Fran has played for six years and is at an ideal age (he was 27). He's young and yet has the full experience at quarterback.

"Fran has a particular quality that makes him better than the others. When a play is broken he can get out and complete the pass. All top quarterbacks must have the ability to get hurried and still complete their pass. Fran has it."

The Fran Tarkenton who came to New York in 1967 was not the same youngster who came out of the University of Georgia six years earlier. Fran was more mature and worldly wise. He had put to good use his degree in business administration and was a highly successful businessman as well as a top quarterback. As soon as the trade was announced, many New York-based organizations contacted Fran for endorsements. He could have made a great deal of money, but he had his own ideas about how he should operate.

"I decided I wasn't going to be sold on every street corner like a bar of soap," he said. "So we've turned down more offers than we've accepted."

Yet Fran's business interests were many and varied. Under the banner of Fran Tarkenton, Inc., he was involved in the following things: the Southeast franchise right for Direction-7, a training course to improve leadership qualities for executives; a 46-unit apartment house in Atlanta; franchise rights to a lucrative gift shop and snack restaurant on the Pennsylvania Turnpike; a chain of smorgasbord restaurants for franchise in 10 northern states.

His business interests have changed some since then, with new enterprises being started, old ones discarded. But through it all, Fran Tarkenton has been immensely successful.

But it was time to get back to the business of quarterbacking a football team. Fran quickly became acquainted with his new teammates and proceeded into the new season with his usual enthusiasm. His Giant debut was strangely similar to his first game with the Vikes years before. Scrambling when he had to and throwing from the pocket whenever he could, Fran led the young New Yorkers to a 37-20 victory over the St. Louis Cardinals, pitching for three touchdowns along the way.

With his usual flair for the dramatic, Fran's Yankee Stadium debut produced a 27-21 victory over the New Orleans Saints. There was little doubt that the Giants were an improved team with Francis at the controls. He had experienced receivers in Joe Morrison, Del Shofner, and Aaron Thomas, and a speed-burner in Homer Jones who was gathering in touchdown passes at a mighty clip.

To everyone's surprise, the Giants were hanging close in the 1967 race. They were in the Century Division of the Eastern Conference that year and chasing the Cleveland Browns for the title. Early in the season,

Francis had engineered a 38-34 upset of the Browns, and their meeting on December 3, might well decide the champion.

The Giants came into the game with a 6-5 mark, one game behind Cleveland's 7-4. After the disastrous 1966 campaign, Giant fans couldn't believe they had a chance.

But the New Yorkers just didn't have the depth. Fran's pass blocking, which had been spotty all season, broke down completely and he was dropped five times for losses of 36 yards. On two other occasions he rushed passes and they were picked off, linebacker Jim Houston returning one 76 yards for the backbreaking score. Cleveland won, 24-14, and the Giants were done.

Detroit beat them the next week before they ended the season with a win over St. Louis. But the 7-7 record and second-place finish was more than anyone expected so soon, and a lot of the credit went to Francis Tarkenton.

The respect still held for Fran by defensive linemen was best expressed by Cleveland end Bill Glass, who said after the Browns' game with the Giants, "We were really pushing out there. When you can down Fran with the ball it's a real thrill. He's so elusive. He's not a normal quarterback and just to get your hands on him means something."

Fran threw the ball 377 times his first year with the Giants, connecting on 204 passes for his career high of 3,088 yards and 29 touchdowns. He completed 54.1 percent of his passes and was intercepted just 16 times. On the ground he was as slippery as ever, running 44 times for 306 yards and an average of 7.0 per carry . . . or per scramble. It was quickly obvious just how much of the Giant offense was attributed to Fran.

To chronicle the remainder of Fran's New York Giant career would almost be like an instant replay of his years with Minnesota. The situations were comparable. The Giants were rebuilding, much as the Vikings were building, and as a consequence, had good weeks and bad weeks, as young and new players attempted to work in with the team.

Fran, too, had his ups and downs, though he was always among the top quarterbacks statistically. The team repeated its 7-7 showing in 1968, finishing a distant second to Dallas in the Capitol Division, to which it had been moved. Fran helped put 294 points on the scoreboard, tossing for 21 touchdowns, but the defense yielded 325, and you can't win with that.

When the 1969 season started, Fran began hearing the old song again. A scrambler won't win a championship. Sure, he'll win some he shouldn't win, but he'll lose some he shouldn't lose, also. Sick and tired of hearing his style maligned, Francis retaliated in a national magazine.

"How can anyone say which type of quarterback can win and which can't?" he said angrily. "To me, that's outmoded thinking. No two quarterbacks are alike, even if they both throw from the pocket. They're still different.

"And no quarterback ever won a championship or even a game by himself. Sure, he's important, but it's the people around him who make the difference. I'm not taking anything away from Johnny Unitas or Bart Starr. They're both great. But you can't ignore the fact that they were surrounded by superb players when they won their championships at Baltimore and Green Bay.

"When Unitas was hurt the Colts won with Gary Cuozzo. When he got hurt, too, they won with a halfback, Tom Matte. When Frank Ryan was with the

Rams they called him a scrambler. When he got to Cleveland with its strong line he won and no one called him a scrambler any more. The difference is in the club, not the quarterback. I don't suppose anyone will admit that a scrambler can win a championship until I win one. It's a strange thing, but I'm still the only quarterback they seem to classify as a scrambler.

"You know," Fran continued, "when you get right down to it, no team wins without a good defense. Namath is a great one, but he couldn't do it until the Jets' defense developed. And how about Starr? When the Packer defense began slipping, the team dipped to 6-7-1, no matter what Bart did. You don't need a great offense to win a championship but a great defense is a must."

A great defense was something the Giants were known for in the late '50's and early '60's. But now the defensive team was made up of untried rookies, journeyman players, and some aging veterans. They just couldn't put it together for more than a week or two at a time.

In '69, the Giants flip-flopped back to the Century Division and found themselves chasing the Browns once more. The team hadn't won a single game in the exhibition season, with the results that head coach Allie Sherman was fired and former Giant fullback Alex Webster took his place. With a new coach, the New Yorkers never quite got organized and finished with a 6-8 mark. And once again the defense yielded more points than the offense could produce.

Fran had another good year and still had his boosters. Veteran defensive back Bruce Maher, traded to the Giants from the Lions, had nothing but praise for his new teammate.

"I played against Fran a lot when he was with Minnesota and I was with Detroit," said Maher, "and I don't know a quarterback any of us feared more. He had this special ability to move the club in the final two minutes, some kind of instinct that tells him just where a defense will be the most vulnerable."

A week after Maher's statement Fran showed just what he meant, bringing the Giants from behind in the final 48 seconds for a 24-21 win against Pittsburgh.

The Giants had a scare in the spring of 1970. They thought they might lose their quarterback to another game—politics. That's right. The ever-popular Tarkenton was invited to run for Lieutenant Governor in his home state of Georgia. But figuring the time wasn't right, Francis politely declined, then went on to say that he was really excited about the season.

That was the year the Giants went into the multiple-formation business. "We're going to be using things like the stacked-I, double wings, and the moving pocket," Fran explained. "It's the real trend in pro football and it's happening now."

And when former quarterback Y. A. Tittle explained the I-formation, it sounded like something that could only work with a Fran Tarkenton-type at the helm. "To run the 'I,'" said Y. A., "you need a back who can catch passes and a quarterback who can sprint out to either side."

Although football still ranked as number one with him, Fran had goals and interests that extended well beyond the gridiron. His various business interests were still quite successful, and he was involved in several educational ventures, which included an electronic tutoring service, and training the disadvantaged for industry. He was truly a concerned citizen.

"I want to be a factor in the running of my city, my state, and my country," he said. "Everyone has to be involved in politics, even if he doesn't run for office. I don't think you can always stand on the sidelines.

"Some people might say I've got too many business interests and it takes away from my football. So far I've managed to keep them apart. My policy has always been from January to mid-June to go full gun producing business for my companies. Then they have to go it themselves. From mid-June on I'm a football player.

"I find I have to be productive and fulfill myself, and that's why my sole purpose in life isn't just to play football. That way, it would be a very short life. But I still like being a football player and I still want to win a championship."

Fran and the Giants almost did just that in 1970. The team started badly, dropping its first three games, and it looked as if they were going nowhere. Then came a victory, then another, and another. Suddenly, the Giants were moving.

Francis was his usual sharp self, only this year he had help. Ron Johnson, a second-year halfback from Michigan, who had been acquired in a trade with Cleveland, was suddenly playing like a superstar, providing the giants with a quick, yard-gaining runner they'd needed. Clifton McNeil, another acquisition, was a receiver of all-pro caliber. And most importantly, the defense was improving rapidly.

In a game against the powerful Cowboys in early November, Francis did his magic act again. The Giants were trailing late in the game. But a circus catch by McNeil for 32 yards helped bring the ball from the Giant 27 to the Cowboy 13. On the next play, McNeil and Johnson lined up on the same side of the field, ran a crossing pattern, and Fran hit Johnson for a touchdown, giving the Giants a 23-20 lead which they held onto. The team had come back from a 20-9 deficit for its fifth straight victory. Suddenly, the Giants were contenders.

Finally, in the 13th game, the Giants' season crested. Fran had a magnificent afternoon, throwing for three TD's and 242 yards in leading a 34-17 rout over St. Louis. That made the team record 9-4. All they had to do was win their final game against the Rams and they'd be Eastern Division champs. Veteran center Greg Larson gave much of the credit to Fran.

"Fran's real cool," said Larson. "That's the great thing about him. He's got this whole club playing it his way. In other words, he's taken command. When Fran tells us something, we listen."

There were some who said the Giants were in over their heads. Maybe. At any rate, the final game proved to be a fiasco. The Rams came into Yankee Stadium and blew the Giants off the field, 30-3, handing the division title to Dallas. But a 9-5 record was better than anyone imagined.

At the end of the season, certain very revealing statistics on the 10-year career of Fran Tarkenton were made known. For instance, Fran the Scram, the man they said was going to lose his head with his scrambling tactics, had never missed a regular-season game because of an injury. That's a record for durability that few quarterbacks ever could match.

Secondly, at the age of 30, Fran had already thrown 205 touchdown passes, the youngest man ever to achieve that mark. Plus he'd thrown for more yards than any other quarterback had in the same length of time, almost 26,000 yards coming on his aerials. And what was even more amazing, as of 1970 there were only five running backs in the National Conference with more career yards gained on the ground. The only thing he hadn't done was win that elusive championship, and that was one stigma he wanted to shed.

The Giants reported to camp on schedule in 1971 and were getting ready for an exhibition game with Houston when a terse announcement suddenly came out of the camp. Fran Tarkenton had left the team in a contract dispute and was threatening to retire. It took the football world by complete surprise. Fran had never openly had difficulty with the Giant management before.

No details of the jump were given. Then, four days later, Fran reappeared and within an hour had signed a one-year contract. When the whole story broke, it was revealed that the scrambler had asked owner Wellington Mara for a substantial loan in place of a regular contract. It was emphasized that the loan was not for business ventures, but would have been an advantage to Fran as an individual. In other words, his advisors thought it would allow him to manage his financial situation in a better way. It was an unusual request and Mara had said no . . . period.

Fran missed the Houston game and was quick to apologize to his bewildered teammates. "I'm sorry for what I did last weekend," he said, in a public statement. "It was a hasty move and difficult for me to think clearly at the time. My greatest desire is to play football here. I'm happier with the Giants than I've ever been in football. I just want to play.

"I'm sorry for what my actions may have done to the team. I just want to make up for lost time and convince the players I sincerely believe I was wrong."

It was easier said than done. As one Giant player said, "Fran's put himself in a difficult position. He's a heck of a player and he's done a lot for the team. But he walked out on us before a game in Houston and no one has forgotten it."

The entire affair was uncharacteristic of Fran. After all, he'd become more of a national celebrity in New York than he'd been in Minnesota. He had his own TV show, his choice of endorsements, and valuable business contacts. Perhaps his unending quest for an NFL championship was beginning to unnerve him.

At any rate, the Giants tried to play down the entire incident, although trade rumors began to circulate and the team lacked a certain zip it had the season before. Then the injuries began to come, noticeably to super-runner Ron Johnson. Without the fleet halfback in there, the offense lost one of its major assets.

The Giants got off to a bad start and never righted themselves. The offense bogged down without Johnson and the defense became the inconsistent unit of two years earlier. Despite an opening game triumph over Green Bay, there weren't too many high spots. Fran did pull one out against the Atlanta Falcons (now coached by Norm Van Brocklin) by carrying the ball over from the two with just half a minute left.

In late November he threw for his 2,000th completion and ran for his 3,000th yard in the same game against the Steelers, but something just wasn't right. With the team at 4-8-1, Coach Webster decided to play second-string quarterback Randy Johnson in the final game of the year. Fran sat on the bench and watched the Giants lose their ninth of the year.

How similar the situations were. In 1966, Van Brocklin had benched Fran at the end and the QB wound up traded. Now, there was speculation again. Fran himself said he was at a stage in his career where he wanted to be with a contender. He demanded to know the Giants' plans. If they intended to embark on another long-range building program, he wanted out.

"It would be totally ridiculous to keep me around to try to keep the record respectable while they rebuild," Fran said. "I feel I'm in the prime of my quarterbacking life and I want to put that to use with a winner. If they can show me that the team can rebuild without jeopardizing the chance to win now, fine. If not; if they are going to sacrifice for the future I won't like it one bit."

Fran let it be known that there were only a few clubs he'd be willing to go to. If he couldn't have it that way he said he'd retire.

"I can't see playing in Philadelphia or St. Louis, places where they aren't settled," he said. "If I play next year the only way I'd move is to a contender, a club like Minnesota or Baltimore."

Wait a minute! Minnesota? Is that ... it sure was. When Fran left the Vikings in 1966 they were gathering a group of fine players. In fact, his trade to the Giants helped the Vikes build even more. Because of it, they acquired players like running back Clint Jones, offensive tackle Ron Yary, and Guard Ed White. They also had a defensive tackle named Alan Page, who was merely the Most Valuable Player in the entire league in 1971.

In fact, from 1969 to 1971, the Vikings under Coach Bud Grant had won 35 games and lost just seven. They went to the Super Bowl in January of 1970, only to lose to the Kansas City Chiefs. But it was the defense that formed the heart of the Viking game. In 1969, the Minnesota defenders yielded just 133 points in 14 games, the next year 143 and the next 139. The team record during that span was 12-2, 12-2, and 11-3.

Unfortunately, the offense never quite kept pace and the team had faltered in the playoffs in 1970 and 1971. The lack of a top quarterback was a major problem, and that's when Fran's name entered the picture.

Shortly after the Vikes lost their opening playoff game to Dallas, 20-12, in December of 1971, Wellington Mara called Vikings General Manager Jim Finks and asked if he was interested in Tarkenton. Finks said yes, he was, and less than a month later the trade was made. Francis returned to the north, and the Giants got an all-pro receiver in Bob Grim, quarterback Norm Snead, rookie runner Vince Clements, and two draft choices. The price for Fran was again high.

While Fran was "overwhelmed" about going back home, some of the Vikings wondered if they'd given up too much. One of those was Alan Page. Said Alan:

"I really don't think much of the trade. Tarkenton is a good quarterback, but I don't think anyone's that good."

But safety Paul Krause disagreed. "Fran might be just what our offense needs. He's got leadership. He knows football. He's a great thrower and I'm excited about it."

Francis returned to the Vikes with the reputation as one of the game's top QB's. He was among the top five in all-time passing stats, and the others names were Unitas, Starr, Jurgensen, Dawson. So he was in fast company.

Yet as Francis himself said, he was now on the spot. "This is the first time in my career that I'm expected to win. Every other year I was with an underdog. I'll never win another 'upset' in my career. Now only other teams will win upsets if they beat us. If we don't win there's only one place to lay the blame—and that's with me."

Fran was setting mighty high standards, but he felt confident. And when Minnesota opened its 1972 season hosting the Washington Redskins, some 48,000 fans jammed Metropolitan Stadium to welcome Francis home. He received a tremendous standing ovation and the game began.

But things don't always go as expected. Fran moved the Vikes all right, leading them to two touchdowns, with several other drives stalling after long marches. Yet strangely enough, the Viking defense couldn't stop the Skins when it counted. Two fourth-quarter TD's enabled the Skins to take a 24-14 lead. But Fran fought back. He had the Vikes on the Redskin four with a fourth-down play coming up and just minutes remaining in the game.

He took a deep breath in the huddle, then called a screen pass to fullback Bill Brown. It was an unorthodox call, but Fran was gambling. He took the snap, rolled right, then lobbed the ball to Brown, who grabbed it and bowled into the end zone. With 70 seconds left, the Vikes had drawn within three, 24-21.

Fred Cox tried an onsides kick. Eleven Vikings scrambled after the ball, but a Redskin fell on it. Washington then ran out the clock and the game was theirs.

"Up to the time the onsides kick failed I thought we had a chance," a dejected Tarkenton said. "I wanted to win this one so badly."

The stats were unreal. Fran had hit on 18 of 31 passes for 233 yards and two scores. He only ran three times, yet gained 35 yards. The Vikes had 26 first downs to 11 for Washington, 382 total yards to 203 for the Skins. They also ran 79 plays to just 48 for George Allen's club. Yet they lost.

One cynical newsman was heard to comment, "Just

like I figured. Last year we always lost the statistics and won the game. Now we'll win the stats and lose the game. I told you that's what Tarkenton does for you."

So the old stigma lingered on. No one mentioned that the team now lacked a top-flight running back, and had only one really reliable wide receiver in John Gilliam. Or that the defense—for no reason anyone could see—yielded over 100 points more than it had the previous three years. And the number of close games was appalling.

There was a 16-14 loss to Miami; a 19-17 defeat to St. Louis; a 13-10 upset by Chicago; and a 20-17 loss to the 49ers. Make all those wins, including the opener, and the team finishes at 12-2 again. But with those five losses the Vikings were a .500 club, seven wins, seven defeats. It was hard to believe.

"I feel so sorry for you, Francis," said the wife of center Mick Tinglehoff after that first game. A lot of people felt that way during the season. And, ironically, the New York Giants, led by a healthy Ron Johnson and a rejuvenated defense, finished at 8-6.

Statistically, Francis had a great season. He completed 215 of 378 passes for 2,651 yards and a 56.9 percentage. He threw for 18 TD's (compared with a career low of 11 the season before) and had just 13 passes intercepted. And he stayed in the pocket, running just 27 times for 180 yards. Yet there were those who said you still can't win with a scrambler. If only he had come back two years earlier.

The Vikings certainly aren't an old football team. There were nagging minor injuries all year and there are a few veteran players who must be replaced. But all is not lost. The team should still be in contention for a good number of years, and it's unlikely that they'll ever let Francis go again.

So Tark continues his quest. As disappointing as the 1972 season was, Fran has come to terms with himself and can bear the strain. In fact, there are some ways in which he's happier than ever, or let's say more philosophical about the game he plays.

"Sometimes I feel funny playing a children's game in my 30's," he said recently. "But I play for just one simple reason. I love it. Nothing else has ever compared with the ecstasies I get from football. And, conversely, nothing compares to the disappointments. But you get that everywhere. People put too much finality into sports. They all lamented about Jerry West, how he never won a championship. Then he won and what did it do to him? Nothing. He's still the same person.

"I want to win a championship. I want it desperately. It's undoubtedly what I want now more than anything else in the world. But if I don't win I won't kill myself. And if I do win, it won't change me one way or another, though it will make me happier than anything else could—right now. But then again, in a few years, it won't make much difference.

"I'll be out of football then and not too many people will really care if I won a title or not. And I'll be thinking of other things, about myself, my goals, new challenges. There's never any sense in looking back."

DARYLE LAMONICA

The most important event in Daryle Lamonica's football life occurred when he was as far away from the gridiron as he could possibly be. In fact, this great NFL quarterback wasn't even thinking about the gridiron when his fate was being decided for him by the bigwigs who run the game.

It was early January in 1967, and Daryle was pursuing his favorite hobby—hunting. He was prowling alone in the mountains of central California, stalking bobcats. The upcoming football season seemed far, far away. It would be his fifth year in professional ball.

When he did stop and think about his career, it was a troublesome business. For four seasons, Daryle had been the backup quarterback to Jack Kemp with the Buffalo Bills. He saw limited action, and when he thought he performed well enough to merit a start, he always met with disappointment.

But none of that mattered as Daryle walked through the wilderness on that warm January day. He was more concerned with bobcats, and sure enough, one suddenly bolted out from behind a rock near him. Lamonica felled the animal with one sure shot, picked up his quarry, and started home.

When he got there, some of his friends were waiting anxiously. As soon as he was within earshot, they began calling out:

"Hey, Daryle. You're not a Buffalo any more, you're a Raider. If you don't believe us, read it in the newspapers!"

It was true, but unbelievable. Just days before, Buffalo coach Joel Collier had told Daryle that he figured prominently in the team's plans for the upcoming year. That meant a real shot at the starting job. Now, he came home to learn that he had been shipped west for Oakland quarterback Tom Flores and all-pro end Art Powell.

Daryle's first reaction was shock; later bitterness. The coldness of the entire affair upset him greatly. An alumnus of Notre Dame University, Daryle Lamonica has never lost the rah-rah spirit of his college days, and was in a sense ignorant of the ways of professional sports.

But once he accepted the trade and reported to his new team, Daryle Lamonica realized that at the age of 26, he'd be embarking on a whole new phase of his career.

"After I thought about it for awhile," he recalls, "I had to celebrate somehow. So I had that bobcat stuffed and stuck a nameplate on him. I called him 'Raider,' and he's still on the wall of my den today."

There were more surprises in store for Daryle Lamonica. For instance, if someone told him then that he'd be taking a team with an 8-5-1 mark in 1966 to a superseason of 13-1 and a trip to the legendary Super Bowl, he would have said "no way."

But that's exactly what happened. The performance was a real tribute to the confidence and ability of one Daryle Lamonica.

Although he came out of Notre Dame, a school with a winning reputation from the days of Knute Rockne, Daryle was at South Bend during one of the rare periods of decline for the Fighting Irish. He often had to share the quarterback job with other signalcallers and when he did play, had to work with a less than potent team.

Coming out of college, Daryle was in fast company. There were plenty of college quarterbacks throughout the land in 1962. Some other seniors were Terry Baker, Glynn Griffing, and Bill Nelson. Juniors George Mira, Billy Lothridge, Jack Concannon, Pete Beathard, Bill Munson, and Don Trull got a barrel of publicity, while sophs Joe Namath, Roger Staubach, and Craig Morton were also already in the public eye.

Playing with a sub-par Notre Dame team, Daryle found that it took tremendous performance in the East-West all-star game to put him on the map. Even with that, the Big D wasn't drafted until many rounds had passed. It was hardly an encouraging start.

Still, Daryle had a lot of things going for him. Start with size. He's 6-3 and weighs around 218 pounds, ideal for a pro quarterback. But there have been guys as big and bigger who've failed. Then there's the arm. Daryle has the traditional cannon. He can throw. But many super-flingers have not succeeded in cutting the mustard. So to make it as a pro, you've got to have something else.

Perhaps the best word for it is character ... that quality which combines the ability to lead, to play when injured, to inspire others, to think, and to produce. Daryle Lamonica has an abundance of all these things.

Somewhat of a traditionalist, Daryle believes in the old-fashioned virtues of hard work and discipline. Although he's considered one of the new breed of pro quarterbacks, Lamonica's appearance is more reminiscent of the 1950's and early 1960's than present day. He dresses conservatively and wears his hair short. Off the field, he's a loner who'd rather hunt or fish than go partying on the town. Since he's got to lead his team, he feels it's better not to form too many close ties with his teammates. Yet he has their respect.

Daryle Lamonica has always had to work hard in order to achieve his goals. He was born on July 17, 1941, in Fresno, California. The Lamonicas lived on a ranch in the San Joaquin Valley and worked very hard raising peaches. So Daryle spent a great deal of his time outdoors from the first.

His grandfather, Pasquale Lamonica, came to the United States from Italy, but never learned the language. His father, Sam, didn't speak English until he went to school. The family concentrated on working their land and earning their living.

"My dad is Italian and my mom is Irish," Daryle says proudly, "and there's even a little pinch of Cherokee for spunk. But I've got a true Italian temper which my mother taught me to control."

Daryle had an older sister, but no brothers. He had to chip in and help work the ranch's 20 acres at an early age.

"We grew peaches and some apricots," he says, "and I always knew what it was like to work. Sometimes I was out there from sunup to sundown, picking fruit. I might have complained some back then, but I had great parents and was very well disciplined."

It's hard to say which interest came first, sports or hunting, but Daryle had his own BB gun at six and was already learning to handle it safely. He was also fooling around with bat and ball then, but he didn't have that much spare time. Then came another setback, a mild case of polio, which fortunately left him no permanent disability.

Daryle's busy life continued right into his high school years, where he finally got the chance to play football on an organized basis. Since he was already big and strong, the coach at Clovis High School, Lloyd Leest, put Daryle at fullback for two years, where the youngster used his drive and determination to roll over many a prospective tackler. He wasn't the fastest or shiftiest guy in the world, but he got the job done.

Prior to his senior year at Clovis, Daryle came out to practice early one day and began tossing the football around with some of his teammates. Coach Leest suddenly noticed the ease with which the young fullback threw the ball, and he was throwing it for some big distances. The coach was having a quarterback dilemma so he was glad to find another candidate. Daryle agreed to try out and promptly won the job.

"Daryle was always a hard-working kid," said Coach Leest. "When we switched him to quarterback he made real fast progress, but he also did everything he could to improve himself. He jumped rope for his footwork and punched the speed bag to improve his eye-hand coordination. He really had a great deal of self-discipline."

Although Daryle was a four-sport star at Clovis High, it took his conversion to quarterback his senior year for him to attract any widespread attention. It wasn't so much that he was a superplayer then, but he had the size, strength, and versatility, and many college recruiters knew that an athlete like him could be used at a number of positions.

One man who saw the potential early was Tom Meehan, who had been a sportswriter for *The Fresno Bee.* Meehan was also a former marine, police captain, and high school coach, so he had many levels upon which to judge a boy. He began talking to Daryle about Notre Dame when Big D was still a sophomore, and he came to have a great deal of influence on the young footballer's early life.

First of all, Daryle had the primary decision that faces many multi-sport high school stars. He was a baseball standout (many thought it was his best sport at Clovis), playing shortstop and pitching, and he was good enough to get a solid bonus offer (some forty to fifty thousand dollars) from the Chicago Cubs. It was a lot of money for a youngster with Daryle's background to pass up.

"I'll never forget the nights we worked on the trees until 10 or 11 o'clock. It was rough, and while it gave me good disciplinary training, it also made me decide I didn't want to go into farming full time.

"My parents were always good about school. They encouraged me to study hard and always let me stay after school to practice baseball, football, or basketball. They always wanted me to continue my education and that's one reason I decided to pass up the baseball offers. Mr. Meehan also strongly suggested I go to school.

"He told me a lot about Notre Dame and its football traditions, but the real thing that sold me on the school was that the people there were the only ones who didn't offer me something under the table. With some of the shady deals I was listening too, that really made an impression on me. I decided to go."

So Daryle enrolled at South Bend in the fall of 1959. He's never had any regrets, but being the great competitor that he is, he sometimes wonders how he would have fared as a major league baseball player.

"I played high school ball with and against guys like Jim Maloney, Dick Ellsworth, and Wade Blasingame," Daryle relates. "They had similar bonus offers and jumped at them. I guess I'll never know just how I would have done, but in my heart I'll always think I could have made it."

When Daryle arrived at South Bend, Joe Kuharich had just taken over as head coach. And somehow, the entire football program was in a rather mixed-up state, a state of decline. Lamonica went out for the freshman team and won the starting job from 10 other QB candidates. He did well, though there weren't very many other outstanding frosh prospects. One thing was for certain, however, his baseball career was over. Coach Kuharich wouldn't allow him to be a two-sport star.

During the 1960 season, Daryle saw more action on defense than on offense. Playing in the secondary, he was credited with 33 tackles and one interception, which he returned 18 yards. His versatility was evident already. He was the team's top punter, booting 23 times for 861 yards and a 37.4 average. As a quarterback, he threw 31 passes, completing 15 for 242 yards and no scores. He had five intercepted.

But he didn't see that much action in passing situations. George Haffner threw the ball 108 times (completing just 30) and Norb Rascher threw 30 times (completing 11), so the Big D was a part-timer at best. He did scramble some 26 times, gaining 73 yards, showing his size and strength. Both other QB's were credited with minus yardage for the season. Daryle also scored three times on the ground.

It was a frustrating season in more ways than one. Notre Dame had one of the greatest winning traditions of any school in the country, yet finished the 1960 season with just two wins and eight big losses, for one of the poorest records in the school's history. Still, the optimistic Lamonica looked to 1961 with his usual enthusiasm.

Kuharich had a few more ballplayers that year and was concerned about putting the whole team together. There just wasn't that much time for him to work with his quarterback. Daryle himself was to say later that "I never had a quarterback coach at Notre Dame." Much of his work was done on his own.

He was officially listed as the starter, but in truth was again an alternate signalcaller. Frank Budka saw as much action as Lamonica and strangely enough, Kuharich leaned toward Budka in passing situations. Lamonica, with his strength and balance, did most of the running from the signalcalling slot.

The Irish were better in 1961, but not that much better. They were a .500 team, winning five of 10 games. Since Daryle was not a regular and the team didn't win big, there was a marked lack of national recognition. Notre Dame quarterbacks usually have a countrywide reputation; Daryle was simply in the right place at the wrong time.

One story on Daryle did appear in the *Chicago Daily News*. It called Daryle a right-handed quarterback who calls his plays left-handed, citing the unusual number of plays that Daryle ran through the left side of his offensive line. Kuharich simply said it was a matter of game plan, and Daryle said nothing except that his fullbacks liked to run to the left better than the right.

Once again it's necessary to turn to the statistics to get the full picture of Daryle's 1961 season. He passed the ball just 52 times, completing 20 for 300 yards and two scores. He had four passes picked off. Budka, by contrast, threw 95 times, completing 40 for 646 yards and three scores. But he had a big 14 of his throws intercepted.

Rushing, Daryle had 135 yards on 44 carries, compared to Budka's 20 yards on 30 carries, so there is a big difference. Defensively, Daryle had another fine year, making 29 tackles, intercepting two passes for 54 yards returned, and breaking up five other pass attempts. He also punted 29 times for 1,113 yards and a 38.4 average. But he vowed to capture the number one quarterback job his senior year and produce.

"I never gave up at Notre Dame," he confessed later. "Sure, I hated losing and in that sense it was the school of hard knocks for me. But the experience made me a better competitor. There were some real problems, but none of the guys got down or became complacent. That's because of the winning spirit at Notre Dame. It was there even when we were losing. Just to hear the fight song always got the blood running fast in my veins. It kind of grows on you, gets bigger and bigger. It was really in my blood when I was a senior and has stayed there ever since. I still get psyched up when I hear it, so I guess it will be with me until I die."

At the outset of the 1962 season Kuharich called Lamonica and Budka "my two first-string quarterbacks," but it was soon apparent that Daryle had the most all-around ability and would be seeing the majority of the action. At last.

As usual, the Irish had a major league schedule, playing some of the best teams in the land. It wouldn't be easy. But in late September, Notre Dame faced the Sooners of Oklahoma and quickly served notice that the team wouldn't be anyone's patsy this year.

Notre Dame scored in the first half on a 10-play drive engineered by Lamonica. He threw three times and hit on all three during the TD march. Then at the beginning of the third period, he took the Irish in again, this time driving for 19 plays, 17 on the ground, and eating up more than 11 minutes on the clock. He completed passes on the two non-running plays.

The score was 13-7 in favor of Notre Dame with about three minutes left. The Irish had the ball and Daryle hoped to eat up the clock. Then he made a mistake. He kept it on a roll-out play and fumbled. Oklahoma recovered.

Daryle looked to the sidelines. He expected a defensive specialist to come in and take his place. But Kuharich motioned for him to stay in at safety.

Oklahoma quarterback Dick Smith wanted to hit the Irish fast. He called a trick play, making eligible tackle Ralph Neely his primary receiver. Smith dropped back and fired over the middle toward Neely. Suddenly, there was number "3," Daryle Lamonica, cutting in front of the bigger man and intercepting the ball. Daryle had almost fumbled the game away. Now he saved it. This time he ran out the clock, and Notre Dame had its first win of the year.

"Daryle analyzed that play perfectly," said Coach Kuharich after the game. "In fact, he was an outstanding performer all afternoon. On both touchdown drives his play selection was excellent. He picked all the right holes, passed when he had to, and hit on all five throws. We weren't as fast or experienced as they were and ball control was our only chance. Daryle gave that to us."

A week later the Irish rolled into Philadelphia to meet favored Navy at Municipal Stadium. The Middies were led by sophomore sensation Roger Staubach, and the publicity received by the Jolly Roger clearly outshadowed that garnered by Daryle Lamonica.

But it was Lamonica who drew first blood in the second period. Daryle directed a 65-yard scoring drive, eating up 17 plays, all on the ground, and climaxing it with a one-yard plunge for the score. That made it 7-0.

Playing on a rainy, wind-swept field that made passing extremely difficult. Navy was held in check by the Irish defense well into the third period. Navy hadn't gotten a single first down and had been unable to penetrate Notre Dame territory when Staubach finally went to work. He directed his club on a 56-yard TD drive, spearheaded by the running of halfback John Sai, who scored from the four. But the try for a two-point conversion fell short as Staubach tried to scramble after an aborted passing attempt.

With the score at 7-6, the crucial fourth quarter began. The weather kept getting worse. Navy drove to the one, only to fumble. The Irish took over, but fumbled it right back. Then Staubach plunged over for the TD. The extra point try failed again and the Middies held a 12-7 lead. That wasn't too safe, so they decided to gamble.

Hoping to take advantage of the slippery field, the Middies tried an onsides kick. They figured they'd have just as good a chance as the Irish to grab the slippery pigskin, and if they did, they'd be in a great position to put the game on ice. There was a wild scramble, and when the bodies unpiled, a Notre Dame player was hugging the football at the Navy 45.

Daryle came on the field, figuring Navy would be unnerved by the gamble that had failed. He wanted to hit fast. Taking the snap, Daryle dropped straight back on the slippery turf, set his footing, and hurled a long pass toward the goal line. Flanker Dennis Phillips outraced two Navy defenders to the spot where the ball was waiting. He grabbed it and rolled into the end zone for a score. A try for two points fell short, but Notre Dame had retaken the lead, 13-12.

Staubach, wary of the slippery grass, tried throwing from the shotgun formation but the Irish defense rose to the occasion. Navy punted and Notre Dame took over on its own 27.

Now Lamonica wanted to eat up the clock. He stuck to the ground and started his team driving. Dan Hogan sparked the drive with a key 24-yard run. Then, on a trick play, Lamonica flipped a 19-yard pass to second-string quarterback Frank Budka that carried to the one. On the next play, the Big D just lowered his head and plunged across the goal line for his second score of the day. The kick by Ed Rutkowski split the upright and Notre Dame had won it, 20-12.

Lamonica had clearly outplayed his Navy rival. Keeping his footing when Staubach couldn't, Daryle completed three of his six passes for 76 yards. Staubach, by contrast, hit on just five of 10 for 57 yards. It was another upset and the one that finally got Lamonica's name in the national spotlight.

A week later, Lamonica struck again, this time going to the air on a dry field and against a solid Pittsburgh team. The Irish won, 43-22, as Daryle directed his club to three first-period touchdowns by producing on three crucial fourth-down calls. He led TD marches in each of the three periods to complete the scoring.

In all, Daryle completed 17 of 27 passes for 214 yards and four big touchdowns. Just one of his passes was picked off. Daryle suddenly found himself named United Press International Back of the Week in the midwest.

"Daryle was just marvelous against Pitt," Kuharich

said a few days later. "I think his passing is improving every week and one reason is that he's taking that second and third look before releasing the football.

"He's also been particularly effective on rollouts because he's holding the ball longer and thoroughly confusing the defenses."

In the Pittsburgh game, Daryle and end Jim Kelly set a school record by hooking up on 11 of the 17 completions. It had taken three years, but Lamonica was finally doing what he knew he could do all along.

There were some lowpoints, of course, losses to Purdue and Southern Cal among others, but the Irish were holding their own without a real powerful or balanced team. Another big game against Iowa started giving Daryle definite pro credentials. Up to then, not too many scouts had really noticed the big guy.

But against Iowa, Daryle not only completed 10 of 19 passes for 144 yards and a score, but he ran for 85 yards on option plays. On one play, Daryle dropped back to pass, seemed trapped by the Hawkeye rusher, but rolled to his right, reversed his field, and ran 27 big yards for a score.

The win over Iowa gave the team a 5-4 record on the year and their fourth straight victory after a slow start. Everyone wanted to win the finale against Southern Cal to give the club a winning year, but it wasn't to be. USC topped the Irish in a hard-fought game, giving Notre Dame its second 5-5 season in a row.

Daryle had by far his best season statistically. He had thrown 128 times, completing half of them (64) for 821 yards and six TD's. He scored four times on the ground, punted 49 times for 1,789 yards, and rushed for 145 additional yards. And he still found time to intercept an enemy aerial, though he no longer played defense on a regular basis. He was named on several all-America squads and finally got a measure of satisfaction for his three years of toil.

Because of his fine season, Daryle was selected to play in the annual East-West Shrine game, pitting some of the best college players in America against each other. Big Sonny Gibbs was slated to quarterback the South. For awhile, no one was sure who'd get the starting nod for the North.

The North coach was Ara Parseghian of Northwestern. He came to camp to meet his players and after one practice knew who his starting signalcaller would be.

"I'll never forget Coach Parseghian," Lamonica says. "He came up to me after that first practice and said, 'Daryle, the moment you entered Notre Dame you became a winner. I know you can win for us. You're my quarterback and I want you to be ready.' That's all I needed to hear. There was just something about the man that made you believe. When I heard that Notre Dame hired him three years later it was like it had to happen. He was made for Notre Dame. I only wish I could have played for him."

The game was a wide-open affair. Both quarterbacks came out firing and were connecting with their receivers. Daryle was cool and confident, following Parseghian's game plan perfectly. But the west squad, coached by USC's Johnny McKay, was a power-packed club and wouldn't be intimidated. In fact, they rallied late in the game and led by a point, 19-18, with a little over two minutes to go. The East had the ball on its own 15. With 85 yards between ball and end zone, it looked bleak. Daryle called time out and came to the sideline.

"Coach Parseghian put both his hands on my shoulders and looked me straight in the eye," he recalls. "He said, 'Look you're a pro now. You've got the time and can still win this thing. If you need help, I'll send it in to you. But I know you can take this club in. I know it.'

"The man had me so charged up that I would have run through a brick wall for him."

That wasn't necessary. Using the clock like a true veteran, Daryle completed six clutch passes and marched his team downfield. With the ball at the two and seconds remaining, Iowa's Larry Ferguson bowled into the end zone and the East had won it, 25-19.

Daryle had been outstanding. He completed a sensational 20 of 28 passes for 347 yards and three touchdowns on that December afternoon, and at the game's end he was named the Most Valuable Player. It had been one of the highlights of his college career, since it proved he could go with the best.

The mutual admiration society between Daryle and Ara Parseghian didn't end with the East-West game. When Parseghian had Notre Dame back in the national spotlight in 1964, a group of reporters began praising the new Irish signalcaller, John Huarte. Many adjectives were bantered around, calling Huarte great, or sensational, or terrific. Then one writer called him the best Notre Dame passer since Johnny Lujack, who had played for the Irish some 15 years earlier.

Parseghian looked up, and without hesitating, said, "I think you guys missed someone. What about Daryle Lamonica? I thought he was terrific when he played here."

As for Daryle, he began looking past his East-West triumph to the upcoming pro draft, which now interested him more than ever before.

"I think my strong points are leadership ability and the ability to learn quickly," he told reporters. "I know

I'll have some handicaps as a pro. First of all, we didn't have a quarterback coach at Notre Dame, so I was left pretty much on my own to learn and improve. Plus we didn't use any checkoffs (audibles) at the line and I know that's a big part of the pro game.

"But I'm confident and know I'll learn, and I'm really itching to get started. Yes, I'm counting on pro football being my career for a good few years at least."

Then the draft came and with it a disappointment. Daryle wasn't picked until the twelfth round by Green Bay of the NFL, and the twenty-second round by Buffalo of the AFL. Quarterbacks expected to make it are generally chosen a lot earlier. So once again he'd have to buck the odds and win a spot for himself. But first he'd have to decide just where he wanted to play.

At first glance, the Packers seemed like the logical team. Green Bay was building a dynasty under Vince Lombardi and the Pack looked as if it would be on top for a long time to come. Buffalo, on the other hand, was also a crack team, one of the better clubs in the new American League. Yet the AFL had only been in existence since 1960, and some people still thought the new league wouldn't survive.

Daryle began surveying the situation. "First of all, I always was a Green Bay fan. Even at Notre Dame I sort of idolized that club, their style and their spirit. In some ways, they were a lot like Notre Dame.

"But when they drafted me, I started to think twice. After all, the Packers had Bart Starr at quarterback. He was already a top passer and was going to be round for a good few years. I figured Lombardi would put me on the bench and that would be it.

"Buffalo, on the other hand, seemed like an up-and-coming team, but one unsettled at quarterback. Jack Kemp had already joined the team and he had experience. But I thought I'd have a better chance of playing behind him as opposed to Starr."

Daryle's decision was helped by the fact that the Packers didn't show any real interest in signing him. So he contacted the Bills to see what they had to offer. Although the two leagues were already bidding for top talent, Daryle wasn't aware of the intricacies of the big money and he didn't get any kind of agent or lawyer to represent him.

"Buffalo offered me $10,000 to sign," he recalls now, almost laughingly. "I figured I'd be real smart. I'd ask for $12,000, then sign for $11,000. That way, I figured I'd squeeze an extra $1,000 out of them. So I made my request and they gave me the $12,000 without another word.

"It wasn't until after that when I learned some free agents were signing for as much as $15,000. So I really came out on the short end of the stick."

When Daryle reported to the Bills in the autumn of 1963, it was obvious that Kemp was number one and Daryle's immediate role would be that of a back-up. That suited him fine. Most people acknowledged that it took several years for a pro quarterback to develop and Daryle figured he'd learn by watching and practicing with the club. The more playing time he got, the better. But he didn't come into the pros with a big head, figuring he should be number one right from the start.

Since the Bills were still building their offense under Kemp's direction, Daryle played sparingly in the exhibition games, though he was working as the team's regular punter and doing a nice job. He got in an exhibition game against Kansas City and brought his team out of the huddle.

"I remember setting up for the snap behind center. I looked up and saw their linebacker, E. J. Holub, staring at me across the line. Suddenly, he starts yelling, 'Rookie, rookie. Let's get him good.' I looked around and I was the only rookie in the lineup. It kind of shook me up a bit, but I recovered and later threw a touchdown pass against them. My first. But it gave me a good idea right then and there that pro football is a battle for survival. You can't let anyone intimidate you and you can't let them shake you up. If you do, you're done."

Daryle didn't see any sustained action in 1963. The Bills were in a dogfight with Boston for the Eastern Division title and they stuck with the veteran Kemp, a quarterback with some limitations, but a fine leader and proven winner. When the season ended, Buffalo and Boston were tied with identical 7-6-1 records. Kemp went all the way in the playoff game. Boston won it, 26-8.

As for Daryle, he was in long enough to complete 33 of 71 passes for 437 yards and three TD's. He remained the team's regular punter and booted the ball 52 times for a 40.1 average, a major league performance. Just four of his passes were picked off during the year, and that showed he was being careful, avoiding the common rookie mistake of throwing too soon or firing into a crowd.

The next year the Bills really put it together, and Daryle was a big part of it. The team scored 400 points, gave up just 242, and rolled to an impressive 12-2 record. This time Daryle was in the thick of the action. Coach Lou Saban relieved him of his punting duties so he could concentrate on quarterbacking, and Saban didn't hesitate to use his young signalcaller. Kemp started all 14 games, but whenever the veteran showed signs of being off his game, Daryle was shuttled into the action. And he performed admirably.

Nine times in all Daryle came into play. Sometimes the game was already won, sometimes the outcome still in doubt. But it didn't matter to him. He played well no matter how much pressure there was. Many Buffalo fans loved Daryle. Whenever Kemp showed signs of faltering, chants of WE WANT LAMONICA came cascading down from the bleachers at the ancient park. And they were well deserved.

In the nine games in which he played, Daryle completed 55 of 128 passes for a big 1,337 yards. He threw for six touchdowns and was intercepted eight times. His completion percentage of 43.0 was low, but his yardage was high. He had striking power and he always knew where that end zone was.

Kemp went most of the way in the title game against San Diego that year, and led the Bills to a 20-7 triumph. Buffalo had become American Football League champions and Daryle Lamonica felt he played a big part of it. He didn't feel as if he were freeloading when he accepted that championship ring.

Daryle enjoyed his off-season. He felt as if he had made a breakthrough as a pro quarterback in his second season. This put him ahead of even his own schedule. He hoped to play even more in 1965.

"When I got to training camp that year," Daryle recalls, "Coach Saban told both Jack (Kemp) and myself that he would decide on his starter by watching us in the exhibition games. I figured I had a real shot and put out more than ever in training camp.

"We did well as a team in the preseason and I think even impartial observers would say that I had the better exhibition season in every respect. But when we opened, Jack was still the quarterback. Coach Saban gave me a lot of reasons, saying that Kemp was more experienced and stuff like that. I didn't agree with his thinking, but the team continued to win and I really couldn't complain."

Kemp had one of his best years in '65. In fact, when it ended, he was voted the Most Valuable Player in the league. As a consequence, Daryle saw even less action than he had his rookie season. He was in long enough to throw just 70 passes, completing 29 for a poor 41.4 percent. His throws gained just 376 yards and he tossed for just three scores. Nevertheless, Daryle retained his confidence. Buffalo vice president Jack Horrigan tells a story about the time he sent Kemp and Lamonica to speak at the same sports banquet together.

"They went off to the banquet all smiles, but when they returned, Jack was really mad," recalls Horrigan. "It seems that Daryle stood up and told everyone that he was a damned good quarterback and that he was really a help to Kemp. Because he was waiting in the wings, he told them, Jack really had to hustle to stay ahead of him. Daryle couldn't understand why Kemp was mad. As far as he (Lamonica) was concerned, he was just telling the truth. That's what I call confidence."

But confidence alone couldn't net Daryle the starting job. Buffalo finished the '65 season with a 10-3-1 mark, then whipped San Diego again, 23-0, to take another title. So it was natural that Kemp was still at the helm when 1966 rolled around. And by then Daryle was really getting restless.

It showed on the sidelines, where Daryle never sat down during games. He paced relentlessly, as if he were playing his own private game by himself. In fact, he admitted that he used to call every play as if he were in the game then see how his choices coincided with Kemp's.

He also saw fit to defend himself against certain criticisms, one of which described him as a running quarterback, a reputation he had since his days at Notre Dame.

"I don't like to be called a running quarterback," he said. "Whenever I relieve Jack in a game it's because our passing offense is sputtering. Sometimes I felt running and controlling the ball was the best solution for that particular situation. But I have confidence that I can pass with the best of them.

"My short passing game needs work, but I'm the first to admit it. I was pulling away from the line of scrimmage after I took the snap and making myself set up off balance. My stride was also too long when I threw and my ball often took off when I tried to throw short.

"Sometimes I was setting up too deep in the pocket, taking nine or 10 yards before throwing instead of the seven or eight I should have been taking. But the coaches have helped me and I hope to play more in 1966."

The Bills got a new coach that year. Assistant Joel Collier took over for Saban, who moved on to Denver. Collier was familiar with the team personnel and relied on the same cast of characters which had brought two consecutive titles to Buffalo. And that cast didn't include Daryle Lamonica. Daryle was again nestled snugly behind Kemp and seeing little action. By November, Daryle's restlessness was turning to discontent. He was tired of being the heir apparent. He wanted action and he wanted it soon.

In late November, the Bills traveled to Oakland to play the Raiders and Daryle got talking to one of the local reporters. The next day his comments worked their way back to Buffalo.

"Sure I'd love to be traded if I could get a shot as a

starter," Daryle was quoted as saying. "It's tough to be on the bench week in and week out, not knowing how much playing time you'll get, if any at all. It's gotten so bad that I've gone up to the coach in the middle of a game and asked when he's putting me in. But I never seem to get an answer."

Later, Daryle said the remarks were printed out of context, that he was happy in Buffalo. But there were some trade rumors in the wind, and he added:

"It's every quarterback's ambition to be number one. If it isn't, he shouldn't be playing football. Jack and I are friends, but he knows I'm after his position. And knowing I'm after it has helped him become a better quarterback."

In the nearly four years that Daryle had been with Buffalo, he started only twice. In October of '66, he helped the Bills salvage a late tie with San Diego, then asked Collier directly if the job didn't earn him another start. The coach didn't answer, and the next week Kemp was back at the helm.

There was an added incentive during that 1966 season. The two football leagues were very close to a merger and the AFL champ would meet the NFL title holder in a world's championship game to be known as the Super Bowl. When the Bills took another Eastern title with a 9-4-1 record, it looked as if they might make it. But it wasn't to be. The Kansas City Chiefs whipped Buffalo, 31-7, and went on to take their drubbing from Green Bay in that first dream game.

By now, Lamonica's statistics were becoming alarmingly repetitious. He had thrown 84 passes, completed 33 for 549 yards and four scores. That was no longer satisfactory for Daryle. He went home and did a lot of thinking. He considered demanding to be traded, but that kind of stuff wasn't really part of his nature. In early March, he went and had a long talk with Collier. The coach apparently assured him he'd have a shot at the number one spot. His old enthusiasm returned quickly.

"I can hardly wait to get back to Buffalo and begin training camp," he said. "I'll admit I was starting to lose some of my interest last year. But I've been working on the speed of my setup and studying films of Bart Starr. He sets up as well as anyone.

"I really hope Jack Kemp comes back in good shape. I want to beat him out at his best—although we still have a friendly rivalry. But I really feel I can lead this team to a championship."

There were some who agreed. The Bills had been standing pat with their basic club for three years and now some of the vets were aging. One writer suggested several major changes if the club was to continue winning. One of them was the installation of Lamonica at quarterback. So things were looking up. That's when Daryle decided to hunt bobcats in the mountains near his Fresno home. When he returned, his friends told him he'd been traded to Oakland.

Reaction to the trade came swiftly. One of the first to comment was Jack Kemp, the man Lamonica could never beat out. "This trade is a coup for Al Davis (general manager of the Raiders)," said Kemp. "Daryle is an above average quarterback with all the qualities— size, strength, and a strong arm. He just needs some playing time, and this is his chance to be a leader.

"I think he'll rise to the occasion with Oakland. As a matter of fact, I think he'll lead the Raiders to a division title."

Jack Horrigan, the Bills' vice president, tried to look at it through the eyes of his coach.

"Coach Collier felt Daryle was weak on medium-length passes. He just didn't think that Daryle had advanced as much as he should have. Plus he felt we could win another title with Powell."

Powell was Art Powell, an all-pro wide receiver. He and quarterback Tom Flores had come to Buffalo in exchange for Daryle. One Oakland writer thought the Raiders had given up too much.

"In one shocking move," he wrote, "the Raiders traded away the number one quarterback they had in the bag, Flores, for the second stringer they hope—and pray—can be a consistent winner, Daryle Lamonica of the Buffalo Bills."

Raider coach John Rauch defended the move. "I'm looking forward to Lamonica's playing here. I'm confident he'll do an excellent job. I've always thought he can become one of the great quarterbacks in pro football."

So the wheels were turning all around. A first glance made it look as if the Raiders had truly made a mistake. The west coast team was quickly building to an AFL power. In both 1965 and 1966, the Raiders finished with identical 8-5-1 marks and seemed on the brink of making a real run at the AFL West title. During the 1966 season, quarterback Flores had emerged to have his finest year, and many thought he was about to become a top signalcaller. Now he was gone, replaced by Lamonica, who'd have to battle another veteran, Cotton Davidson, for the number one spot.

There was a tremendous amount of pressure on Daryle when he reported to his first Raider camp in 1967. Not only did he have to convince his new teammates that he could lead and win, but he had to show the coaches and fans that he was the right man for the job. And that meant learning a whole new offense, a complex offense, and learning it quickly.

"The Raider system is football at its best," he said enthusiastically. "Once it's mastered, there's no defense it can't beat. It's complex, all right, but very explosive.

"If I can recognize the defense quickly, I have the option to call an audible at the line and come up with a gainer."

The young quarterback worked very hard, day and night. There were some low points early in the training season. "I didn't feel like a real leader in the first two scrimmages," he said "I wasn't moving the club, and it was my fault. We had the weapons to make the plays work."

Going to a new team is never easy. And it's even harder for an inexperienced quarterback like Daryle. He had to learn to read his receivers, learn their habits, their different speeds. His throwing style was the same, but he had to make some modifications.

"I've got to drop back deeper here than with Buffalo," he told reporters. "Oakland's pass patterns break later and I can hold the ball longer before releasing. It's a discipline problem, learning to wait until the last possible second."

And when he wasn't practicing on the field, he was studying. Daryle roomed with the veteran Davidson and often kept Cotton up all night, asking questions about the Raider offense and about football in general. By the time the season started, Daryle had won the number one spot and the Raiders were favored to take the crown. Oakland was strong all around. Both lines were big and tough. Clem Daniels and Hewritt Dixon were power runners. The receivers were improving and the defense was as good as they come, especially in the all-important secondary.

The club was just 2-3 in the preseason, but by the time they opened against Denver the Raiders were

ready. Exploding in a way no one really expected, the
big bad Raiders lashed the Broncos at will, winning
51-0. Lamonica was a star right from the first, whip-
ping sure shot passes to his cutting receivers and leading the team without a flaw. The TD passes seemed to
fall from the sky like rockets, hitting their mark with
pinpoint precision. The Big D had finally found a
home.

Lamonica led the Raiders to a 35-7 conquest of Boston the next week, but when the team hosted Kansas
City, they were marked underdogs. That didn't matter
to Daryle. He was cool as a noodle as he pitched the
Raiders to a 23-21 victory, putting the Oaklanders on
top of the Western Division.

Just when things looked brightest, the Raiders hit a
snag. They dropped a 27-14 decision to the New York
Jets in what might have been the first game in football's
most heated rivalry, matching the TD slants of Joe Namath and Daryle Lamonica.

"I had four interceptions," Daryle said. "I thought
two were completions because I didn't see the defender.
The other two were good interceptions. We all suffered
sort of a letdown, but I don't think it will happen
again."

Daryle was right. Although the Raiders were often
underdogs because of their inexperienced quarterback,
they began rolling over the rest of the league. There
was a 24-20 get-even game with Buffalo, then big victories over Boston and San Diego, in which the club
put 99 points on the scoreboard.

The Raiders were 8-1 when they came in to Kansas
City for a Thanksgiving Day showdown. Once again
Lamonica's wrecking crew found themselves 6½-point
underdogs. So Daryle took a deep breath and went to
work.

On the first play from scrimmage, Daryle simply dropped back and whipped a 40-yard completion to Fred Biletnikoff. That opened the flood gates. Before it ended, Daryle had completed 20 of 35 passes for 281 yards and the Raiders had a big, 44-22, victory.

There was another showdown the next week, with the still-potent San Diego Chargers. The game was close in the third period and the Raiders had a third-and-one play at their own 37. Daryle faked a running play to Pete Banaszak, then whipped a 63-yard TD pass to tight end Billy Cannon. He was 21 for 34 that day and the Raiders won, 41-21.

Three more victories followed, including a 38-29 equalizer with the Jets, and the Raiders had themselves a 13-1 season. They were Western Division titleholders, and Daryle Lamonica was the talk of all football.

In four years at Buffalo, Daryle had a total of 150 completions in 353 attempts and 16 touchdowns. Now, in a single season as a regular, he had completed 220 of 425 passes for 3,228 yards and a 51.3 percentage. He led the AFL and set a club record with 30 touchdown passes. And to top it all off, he was named the Most Valuable Player in the league.

"Daryle gave our offense the confidence it needed," said Coach Rauch, himself a former pro quarterback. "Even when we were getting bad breaks he kept his head and kept the offense moving."

But perhaps the thing which made Daryle happiest, or at least gave him the most satisfaction, was a piece of verse that was being chanted all over Buffalo, where the Bills had faltered to a 4-10 record. The couplet was coined by Jack Horrigan, who always liked Daryle:

> *All we want for Hanukah,*
> *Is Oakland to return Lamonica.*

That wasn't about to happen. The Raiders had their man and he had some more business to attend to, like leading a 40-7 romp over Houston for the American Football League Championship. Now the Raiders would prepare for the upcoming Super Bowl clash. They would face the powerful Green Bay Packers, who had defeated the Rams and Cowboys to earn their super shot. In the first Super Bowl the season before, the devastating Packers had whipped the Chiefs, 35-10. Now they were heavy favorites to do the same thing to the Raiders.

"Green Bay can be beaten," said Daryle with his usual confidence. "But it will take 60 minutes of tough football and no mistakes. Kansas City made some errors last year, got behind, then lost its cool. We can't let that happen, because the Packers are always ready to pounce."

The game was played in Miami's Orange Bowl on January 14, 1968. Daryle was nervous, but confident. Oakland received the opening kickoff and Daryle tried to establish a running game. He wanted to give his line confidence that they could handle the Packers. But Green Bay was ready and stopped the Raiders cold. After a punt, the Packers drove down to the Oakland 32, and Don Chandler came on to book a 39-yard field goal. Green Bay led, 3-0, and had taken command of the inside game on the line.

The same pattern continued. The Packer linebackers were proving to be even faster than the Raiders thought and were shutting off the Oakland running game. By contrast, the Green Bay line was opening holes for Donny Anderson and Ben Wilson, and the Pack kept eating up ground in short bursts. They drove from their own three all the way to the Oakland 13 before the drive stalled. Then Chandler came on to boot another field goal and Green Bay had a 6-0 lead.

Midway in the second period, the Packers had the ball again on their own 38. It was a first and ten play, but instead of calling the expected running play, quarterback Starr faded back to pass. He spotted flanker Boyd Dowler going one-on-one with cornerback Kent McCloughan and let fly. Dowler grabbed the ball alone at the 40 and ran untouched all the way to the end zone. The kick made it 13-0, and many of the 75,000-plus spectators figured the rout was on.

This was the time most teams would fold under the Packer might. But Daryle Lamonica was determined not to let that happen to the Raiders. He had been trying to send his backs around the ends to that point. Now he decided to run right up the middle, and Hewritt Dixon and Pete Banaszak began picking up some good yardage. When they stalled, Daryle began swinging short passes out to the sideline.

The drive carried 55 yards to the Packer 23. Then Daryle dropped straight back to pass. He spotted end Bill Miller heading for the corner of the end zone with big linebacker Dave Robinson a step behind. Ignoring the Packer pass rush, Daryle lofted a perfect pass over Robinson's head and into Miller's arms. The ref raised both hands and the Raiders had broken through. Veteran George Blanda booted the extra point and it was suddenly a ballgame again at 13-7. But minutes before the half ended, Rodger Bird fumbled a Packer punt and Green Bay recovered. Chandler came on to boot a 43-yard field goal, and that made it 16-7 at intermission.

Green Bay had some extra incentive to win on this January day. Their great coach, Vince Lombardi, was stepping down as head man after the game.

"Let's play this last 30 minutes for the old man," said Jerry Kramer in the locker room. "We don't want to let him down now."

Early in the third quarter, the cagey Starr caught the Raider defense napping. Green Bay had a third and one on its own 40, and the Raiders packed in tight. They were warned that Starr liked to surprise opponents in this situation, but they had forgotten in the heat of battle.

Bart faked a plunge with his fullback, then dropped back and threw in the direction of Max McGee, also playing his final game. McGee caught the ball behind safety Bird and raced all the way to the 25 before he was caught from behind. Two more passes brought the ball to the two, and Donny Anderson crashed over for the decisive score. It was 23-7, and the Raiders would have to forget their game plan and go for broke. There were no alternatives left.

Daryle was forced to go to his long passing game, and sure enough, one was picked off. But it was a big one, Herb Adderly grabbing it and lugging it back 60 yards for a touchdown. Another Chandler field goal made it 33-7 before Lamonica flipped his second TD pass to Miller. The final was 33-14, with the Packers once again proving to be the best team in football.

It wasn't a bad day for Daryle. He was 15 of 34 for 186 yards and two scores. But Starr proved he was still the old master and hit the clutch plays to win the game's MVP award.

The loss didn't dampen Daryle's confidence. He and the Raiders were a young team and he figured they'd be back, probably the next season. And before the 1968 campaign starter, the Raiders tore up Daryle's contract and signed him to a new three-year pack calling for something like $200,000. It was a far cry from his original contract with Buffalo five years earlier.

There was little doubt that the Raiders were again a powerhouse in '68. Daryle took up where he left off and the team romped through its first four games. Two losses to San Diego and Kansas City marked the team's only slump, then they rolled again. On November 17, the Raiders met the New York Jets in a game that pitted both divisional leaders. It also marked the continuation of the Lamonica-Namath rivalry.

The two teams were very evenly matched, and when they met, the footballs invariably flew throuth the air with great frequency, the two quarterbacks overshadowing the fine defensive units of both clubs.

It was about as expected, both quarterbacks firing strikes all evening before a prime-time national television audience.

With less than two minutes remaining, the Jets had a 32-29 lead and the football. It was almost nine P.M. in the East (the game was being played at Oakland) and the network had a scheduled special production of *Heidi*, a classic children's story. Instead of running over with the game, network producers figured the Jets had it wrapped up and they cut away to show *Heidi* as scheduled.

Irate fans called their TV stations, and many flipped on their radios. Almost all expected the Jets to run out the clock, but they felt cheated that they'd been cut off unexpectedly. What almost no one counted on was the lightning in the right arm of Daryle Lamonica.

The Jets committed a turnover and Oakland had the ball. Lamonica just dropped back and fired long. BANG! He was on target and the Raiders had the go-ahead score. That wasn't all. When the Jets got the ball again, they promptly turned it over, and Lamonica struck again. In less than two minutes he had put 14 points on the scoreboard, and the Raiders won, 43-32.

Now known as the "Heidi Bowl," the game went down in history as a major network blunder. Never again has a football game been cut off before the final gun. The strong right arm of Daryle Lamonica is one of the main reasons.

Oakland played out its schedule to the tune of a 12-2 record. Daryle was great again, throwing for more than 3,000 yards and hitting on 25 touchdowns. The only problem was that Kansas City also finished at 12-2, and the two clubs had to meet in a playoff to decide the title.

Lamonica settled that one quickly. Going to the air early and often, Daryle obliterated the Chiefs with five touchdown passes and the Raiders won it, 41-6. It was as if he couldn't wait to get at the Jets and their MVP, Joe Namath.

The game was played at New York's Shea Stadium before a screaming throng of more than 62,000 fans, and it quickly turned into a typical Oakland-New York encounter.

As usual, the lead see-sawed back and forth several times. Namath led a fourth-quarter drive that put his club back in front, 27-23, with about two minutes left. Now it was Oakland's turn again, and there were many fans who thought Daryle Lamonica would pull it out. In fact, Daryle himself was confident he could do it.

The Raiders had a first down on their own 24. Daryle called a pass over the middle to his fullback, Hewritt Dixon. He took the snap from center Jim Otto and dropped back. The Jets were charging hard, and he felt again that he had made the right call. It should gain good yardage, he thought.

But when he looked past the onrushing linemen,

Daryle saw that Dixon was covered. He didn't have time to look for a secondary receiver. Then he spotted his halfback, Charlie Smith, who had drifted about 15 or 20 yards out into the right flat. At the last second he tried to get the ball out to Smith, but the pass wobbled and fell several feet behind the receiver.

"I thought it was an incomplete forward pass," Smith said. "So I didn't make a move for the ball."

Jets linebacker Ralph Baker did. He grabbed the football and ran it into the end zone. But whistles were blowing all over the field. No one was quite sure what had happened.

The officials conferred, then agreed that the pass had not gone forward and had to be considered a lateral, which made it a free ball. Baker's recovery was allowed, but not his romp to the end zone. It didn't matter. The Jets had the ball and were able to run out the clock. They won the game and the AFL crown, and two weeks later became the first AFL team to win in the Super Bowl, defeating the Baltimore Colts, 16-7.

It galled the Raiders to think about the loss. They felt they had not only the best team in the AFL, but the best in football, and there were many who agreed. There wasn't a weak spot on the club. As far as Daryle was concerned, the Raiders were the best team. Without intending conceit, he was heard to say, "I'm the number one man on the number one team in all football."

And he continued to defend his attempted pass to Smith. "Sure, I've thought about that one bad play. It may have cost us everything, but I still say it was the right move under the circumstances. A little better execution on my part and it could have turned into a big gainer.

"As far as I'm concerned, our future looks bright.

Maybe next year at this time you'll be asking me about the pass that won the Super Bowl."

In the 1969 opener against Houston, Daryle was off. He completed just nine of 30 for 84 yards and had three intercepted. He heard a new sound coming out of the stands, the sound of boos. Yet the Raiders won it, 21-17, and were started on another successful campaign.

The Raiders were still unbeaten (but tied) five weeks later when they went up against the Buffalo Bills. It may have been the most satisfying day of his career. In the first period he hit Billy Cannon with a 53-yard scoring strike. Minutes later he found Pete Banaszak from the 10.

In the second period he again passed to Banaszak, this time from one yard out. On the next series he drove his club downfield and connected with speedy Warren Wells from the 13. Next it was Fred Biletnikoff from the 16 and Biletnikoff again from the 23. Six scoring passes in all, and every one coming in the first half of play. The Raiders led, 42-7, and veteran George Blanda got to play the second half.

The next week, Daryle did the dramatic again. He got sick—some kind of virus or flu—and he was hospitalized with a fever of 103 degrees. He couldn't hold anything in his stomach and the doctors said that unless his temperature was normal, he couldn't leave the hospital.

On the day of the game, Daryle pulled a number with the thermometer. He held it between his teeth, but not under his tongue. It registered normal and he was released. At the Stadium he tried drinking a 7-Up. It came up. Then he went out on the field to face the Chargers.

If Daryle was sick, it's frightening to think what he

would have done healthy. He completed 19 of 26 passes, hit for three scores, and led his team to a 24-12 win. After the game, a newsman asked him if he was worried about winning the game.

"No," he said quickly. "I knew if I could suit up, I could win."

Win he did, as usual. The Raiders rolled through their schedule again and finished with a 12-1-1 record. Daryle's three-year mark since coming to Oakland rose to 37-4-1, and there was never a quarterback anywhere who could match that.

Statistically, he was over 3,000 yards for the third straight season, and he heaved 34 touchdown passes, becoming the first quarterback to go over the 30 mark twice. His 221 completions were a new personal high and once again he looked forward to leading his team into the playoffs. Plus he was once again the Most Valuable Player in the AFL.

Still, it wasn't an easy year. He had hand and back injuries, a pulled hamstring, bruised ribs, a sore shoulder and sore knee. He said it was his worst year physically. He showed no ill effects in the first round playoff, leading the Raiders to a 56-7 romp of Houston. Now the Raiders had to face their old rivals, the Chiefs.

New Raider Coach John Madden looked forward to the K.C. game. "I think we'll win," he said. "Daryle threw six TD's against Houston so there's no question about him being ready physically, but it should be the usual rough game."

Daryle himself was confident, saying, "I'm a take-charge guy. I can lead this team and I can win. And if we go to the Super Bowl again you'll see a much better quarterback than you saw against Green Bay two years ago."

The game was played in Oakland before a packed

house of cheering fans. They really got high when the Raiders drew first blood in the opening period. Daryle tossed a 22-yard pass to Warren Wells, bringing the ball to the three, and Charlie Smith took it in on the next play.

But the Chiefs came back in the second, Len Dawson setting it up with a 42-yard completion to Frank Pitts. Wendall Hayes scored from the one and the game was deadlocked, 7-7, at halftime.

Then, early in the third quarter, everything went bad at once. First, Daryle smashed his throwing hand against the helmet of defensive end Aaron Brown. The hand swelled, and Daryle left the game for eight minutes. In his absence, George Blanda failed to move the club, and missed a field goal try from the 40. When Blanda threw again, Emmitt Thomas intercepted on his own six.

A few plays later, Dawson connected with Pitts on a long bomb that got the Chiefs out of trouble and led to the go-ahead score. A field goal by Jan Stenerud made it 17-7 in the fourth period.

Fighting off the pain in his hand, Daryle went back in. He threw all right, but didn't seem to have any zip on the ball. The Raiders blew chance after chance, recovering three K.C. fumbles, only to have the Chiefs retaliate via the interception. When it ended, the score was still 17-7, and it was Kansas City that went on to win the Super Bowl game.

And once again people were saying that the best team in football had been eliminated.

Daryle took the blame for the defeat, acknowledging that he couldn't throw that well, but defending Coach Madden's decision to stick with him, rather than Blanda.

"I'm the team's leader. I'm the guy they depend on.

When this is the case you have to go as long as you can go."

There were some other grumblings. Blanda hinted that he should have been allowed to remain in, and flanker Fred Biletnikoff wondered out loud why the ball wasn't thrown his way more often. Then the word came out of Oakland that had the team won, Daryle would have not been able to play in the Super Bowl. The hand was too badly swollen. And he was scratched from the all-star game the week after that. But the damage was done. The Raiders, with their 37-4-1 three-year mark, lost one Super Bowl, and failed to get there on two other occasions. There was bound to be some grumbling.

For the first time there were critical comments on Daryle's quarterbacking, despite a three-year record that was the best in football. "He doesn't listen, doesn't follow the game plan," an anonymous player was quoted as saying. "He thinks he can throw a TD on every play," said another. "He's bomb crazy. He's going to have to tone down if we ever expect to win the big one."

The 1970 season was one of frustration for Daryle. A loss to Cincinnati, a tie with San Diego, and a defeat by Miami left the club at 0-2-1 after three games. And Daryle was already picking up a string of minor injuries that were to dog him all year. Then, suddenly, a new hero emerged.

It was George Blanda, the little-used backup quarterback. Blanda had been in pro ball since 1949. He had had his glory years with the Houston Oilers in the early days of the AFL. Now he kicked, and kicked well, and played a little backup for Lamonica. At the age of 43, Blanda wasn't expected to play too much quarterback.

But in the ensuing five weeks, he became a legend to the geriatric set. Five times in five weeks he came off the bench either to win or to earn a tie with his arm and his leg. He booted a 52-yard field goal to win one, and threw key TD passes to take a couple of more. Lamonica would start, Blanda would relieve, and the fans began to adore ancient George Blanda.

The Raiders finished at 8-4-2 that year, good enough to take their division in the newly merged NFL. Daryle threw for 2,500 yards and had 22 TD tosses. Blanda completed just 29 passes, but six went for scores.

Unfortunately, the playoff story was the same. The Raiders won the first round over Miami, then lost the American Conference title game to Baltimore, 27-17, and were eliminated from Super Bowl consideration once more.

Once again Daryle bore the brunt of the criticism. But, in truth, the Raiders weren't quite the potent football force in 1970 that they'd been before. They had to start rebuilding before the veterans slipped too far. And once again, Daryle's injury list read like a medical report from all over the league. He had, at one time or another, a separated sternum, a bruised shoulder, a jammed wrist, muscle spasms in the back, a bruised Achilles tendon, and (in the title game with the Colts) a groin injury.

The boo-birds criticised everything. It was widely known that Daryle loved to hunt, to get away and relax. By now, he had hunted everywhere and everything, including a safari to Africa. Some saw fit to question the morality of hunting, citing he had bagged some animals on the endangered species list.

"A true sportsman doesn't look at killing in the strictest sense," Daryle said. "No one really enjoys killing. It's the challenge, the excitement. There's danger involved and a charging bull elephant or cape buffalo gives me some of the same feelings I get when a defensive lineman charges at me. I really don't know the answer, but it's my life. It's something I really enjoy. What's good for me might not be good for another human being."

But while some people were harping on Daryle's fondness for hunting, others pointed out that the quarterback was also very active in something called the Presidential Classroom for Young Americans. It was a six-week school, meeting in Washington, with a student body of high school students from every state with the potential to be leaders in government. Daryle served as coordinator and moderator for the seminars, which included guest instructors from all the top levels of government.

"It's a way of helping the youth of our country and is something I've always wanted to do," he said. "I've spoken to many young people's groups the past several years, but this is something different, and it's enabled me to learn how really great our educational system is."

So Daryle didn't spend all his spare time hunting. But his main concern was still football. Right from the start of the 1971 season, the fans were down on him. They had a new hero, young Ken Stabler of Alabama, a lefty passer who was up briefly in '69 before personal problems forced him to leave the game. Now he was back and trying for a job. He quickly showed he could move the club.

In an exhibition game against the 49ers, Daryle was booed every time he came out on the field. He completed just four of nine passes for 59 yards, while Stabler connected on 10 of 14 for 162. It was obvious which quarterback the fans favored.

But it was also obvious which quarterback would

have to produce if the Raiders were going to win. And his name was Daryle Lamonica.

The team lost its opener, then came back to win five straight. Daryle was starting, but he was generally relieved at some point by either Blanda or Stabler.

In an October game against the lowly Philadelphia Eagles, Stabler started and hit 11 of 15 passes in the first half. Yet the Eagles led, 10-0. Daryle relieved this time and pitched the Raiders to a 34-10 victory.

But there were more injuries. Daryle had hand miseries again, and they contributed to his seeing less action than any time since coming over to Oakland. Besides the bad hand, he had a hamstring pull and various other muscle ills. Yet Daryle was not the kind of guy who liked sitting down, under any circumstances. As he once said, "If I can pull on the uniform, I can win the game."

With Stabler seeing some starting action in 1971, Daryle began feeling a kind of restlessness he hadn't known since his Buffalo days.

"I'll never forget my days on the bench behind Jack Kemp," Daryle told the Oakland press that year. "When I came here I said 'Never again!' I don't like to sit on the bench and I don't intend to sit."

Games like the Philly encounter showed it was still Lamonica who put the points up. But Stabler was coming. The Oakland coaching staff may eventually have to choose between them.

The Raiders hung on through 10 games with a 7-1-2 record. It looked like another divisional crown. But, suddenly and without warning, the team collapsed, losing to Baltimore, Atlanta, and Kansas City on successive weekends. The K. C. game dropped the Raiders into second place. The Chiefs finished at 10-3-1, the

Raiders at 8-4-2. Oakland was out of the playoffs for the first time since 1967.

There were two reasons for this. First of all, the Raiders, as a team, were changing. The club missed wide receiver Warren Wells, who was in trouble with the law. Wells had grabbed 36 touchdown passes during the preceding three years. Moreover, the entire defensive line was showing signs of age and Al Davis and John Madden were beginning to rebuild. Injuries to the running backs further slowed the club, and then it was revealed that Daryle's hand injury had been much more serious than anyone thought.

In fact, it was learned that his football career was in jeopardy. It seemed that Daryle had hurt the hand in the first league game of the season, hitting it on the face mask of a charging lineman. There were torn tendons that could only be restored with surgery.

"I never alibied or made excuses," he said after the season. "I just don't believe in that. Not even Coach Madden really knew how much pain I was in during those weeks."

Daryle had been taking pain-killers throughout the season. When he showed the hand to reporters before his scheduled operation, the knuckle of his little finger was badly swollen and deformed. Witnesses said the deformity appeared permanent.

"You can't grip a ball properly with this kind of thing," Daryle explained. "There's a great deal of pressure applied with the little finger when you throw, and I couldn't release properly."

Daryle completed just 118 of 242 passes in 1971, reflecting the injury and loss of playing time. He passed for just 1,717 yards and 16 touchdowns. Those aren't normal Lamonica stats.

The operation was performed in early 1972 by Doctor Robert Rosenfeld of Los Angeles, who repaired the tendons, removed some cartilage and pronounced the surgery successful.

When 1972 rolled around, Daryle had his old enthusiasm back, though Coach Madden acknowledged that Stabler was going to be given a full shot at winning the job. Trade rumors were heard all over the place involving both players, but the Raider management insisted that both would remain with the club.

Daryle admitted that the booing and loss of leadership hurt him. Some said that there was a feud between him and Blanda. Others said that the new zone defenses had taken away Daryle's primary weapon, the long bomb.

In answering his critics, Daryle Lamonica admitted that the zone made it a whole new ballgame for the Raiders. They had to adjust offensively, especially to handling the pass rush.

"Any quarterback who has time to throw can beat any kind of defense," he said. The supreme confidence in his passing had never wavered.

When asked about Daryle as a quarterback in 1972, his first coach, Lou Saban (who had returned to the Bills), was quick to answer.

"I don't believe all this about Daryle being 'the mad bomber' and all that other stuff. Throwing deep seems to be the club's philosophy rather than his. They often seem content to keep trying in the hope that they'll finally break one.

"As far as I'm concerned, Daryle's still a top quarterback and he probably will be for a long time to come."

Not surprisingly, Daryle was still the number one quarterback when the 1972 season opened. Davis and Madden had rebuilt the Raider defense quickly, Marv

Hubbard became a 1,000 rusher, and the rest of the team stayed relatively free of injuries. The Chiefs slipped somewhat, while the Chargers and Broncos were not yet strong enough to challenge for the top spot. The Raiders regained the Western Division AFC title with a 10-3-1 mark.

Daryle saw the majority of action at quarterback, though Madden didn't hesitate to relieve him in certain situations with either Stabler or the aged Blanda. Wells had not returned, and with the emergence of Hubbard as a premier runner, the club didn't throw as much as in the past. But Lamonica had a steady, if not spectacular, season.

He threw the football 281 times, completing 149 for a percentage of 53.0, his best ever. His passes gained 1,998 yards and he whipped 18 TD passes as opposed to 12 interceptions. He was the second leading passer in the conference behind Earl Morrall of Miami, who hadn't played nearly as much.

Once more the Raiders entered the playoffs. Going against the rejuvenated Pittsburgh Steelers, the Raiders looked sloppy. Both defenses dominated the ballgame through three periods. The only scoring was a pair of field goals by the Steelers' Roy Gerela, giving Pitt a 6-0 lead. Through those three periods, Daryle had completed just six of 18 passes for 45 yards. It wasn't a good day, and when the final period began Stabler was in the game.

The Snake, as Stabler is called, did the job, moving the team well and finally breaking free on a 30-yard scramble that gave the Raiders their only touchdown. Blanda's kick made it 7-6 with just minutes remaining.

That's when fate took a hand. Pittsburgh had the ball on its own 40 with five seconds left. It looked as if Oakland was going to pull it out. Steeler QB Terry

Bradshaw fired one over the middle. The ball was deflected by safety Jack Tatum and that appeared to do it. Suddenly, fullback Franco Harris was galloping toward the goal line with the football. He had picked off the deflection and caught the Raiders flatfooted. The play was legal, and in a most dramatic finish, the Steelers had pulled it out, 13-7.

Another season had ended on a frustrating note for Daryle, the Oakland fans, and the club's management. It left the future of the Raiders and Daryle Lamonica somewhat in doubt. Al Davis is not a man to take defeat lightly. He may decide to shake up the club again.

Daryle Lamonica has been a great quarterback. He is still a great quarterback. And he is in the prime of his football life. The last few years have been terribly disappointing. Plagued by injuries and some key losses, the Big D had fallen in esteem in the eyes of many. But with his great confidence and enthusiasm for the game, he's burning to redeem himself and get his team into the Super Bowl once again. Some feel that his team won't be the Oakland Raiders much longer. Maybe, maybe not. A large majority of NFL clubs would love to have Daryle Lamonica.

One thing is for sure. Daryle Lamonica will never again sit the bench behind someone else. In his own heart and mind, he's number one. That's the first prerequisite for greatness. Daryle has that one, and many others as well. And he's proven it, many times over.

STATISTICS

Terry Bradshaw

Team	Year	Att.	Comp.	Pct.	Yds.	TD	Int.	Ave. Gain
Pittsburgh	1970	218	83	.381	1,410	6	24	6.47
Pittsburgh	1971	373	203	.544	2,259	13	22	6.05
Pittsburgh	1972	308	147	.477	1,887	12	12	6.13
Pro Totals 3-years		899	433	.481	5,556	31	58	6.18

Billy Kilmer

Team	Year	Att.	Comp.	Pct.	Yds.	TD	Int.	Ave. Gain
San Francisco	1961	34	19	.559	286	0	4	8.41
San Francisco	1962	13	8	.615	191	1	3	14.69
San Francisco	1963			did not play				
San Francisco	1964	14	8	.571	92	1	1	6.57
San Francisco	1965			did not play				
San Francisco	1966	16	5	.313	84	0	1	5.25
New Orleans	1967	204	97	.475	1,341	6	11	6.57
New Orleans	1968	315	167	.530	2,060	15	17	6.54
New Orleans	1969	360	193	.536	2,532	20	17	7.03
New Orleans	1970	237	135	.570	1,557	6	17	6.57
Washington	1971	306	166	.542	2,221	13	13	7.26
Washington	1972	225	120	.533	1,648	19	11	7.32
Pro Totals 11-years		1,724	918	.532	12,012	81	95	6.97

Daryle Lamonica

Team	Year	Att.	Comp.	Pct.	Yds.	TD	Int.	Ave. Gain
Buffalo	1963	71	33	.465	437	3	4	6.15
Buffalo	1964	128	55	.430	1,137	6	8	8.88
Buffalo	1965	70	29	.414	376	3	6	5.37
Buffalo	1966	84	33	.393	549	4	5	6.54
Oakland	1967	425	220	.513	3,228	30	20	7.59
Oakland	1968	416	206	.495	3,245	25	15	7.80
Oakland	1969	426	221	.519	3,302	34	25	7.75
Oakland	1970	356	179	.503	2,516	22	15	7.07
Oakland	1971	242	118	.488	1,717	16	16	7.09
Oakland	1972	281	149	.530	1,998	18	12	7.11
Pro Totals 10-years		2,499	1,243	.497	18,505	161	126	7.40

Fran Tarkenton

Team	Year	Att.	Comp.	Pct.	Yds.	TD	Int.	Ave. Gain
Minnesota	1961	280	157	.562	1,997	18	17	7.13
Minnesota	1962	329	163	.495	2,595	22	25	7.89
Minnesota	1963	297	170	.572	2,311	15	15	7.78
Minnesota	1964	306	171	.559	2,506	22	11	8.19
Minnesota	1965	329	171	.520	2,609	19	11	7.93
Minnesota	1966	358	192	.536	2,561	17	16	7.15
New York G	1967	377	204	.541	3,088	29	16	8.19
New York G	1968	337	182	.540	2,555	21	12	7.58
New York G	1969	409	220	.538	2,918	23	12	7.13
New York G	1970	389	219	.563	2,777	19	12	7.14
New York G	1971	386	226	.585	2,567	11	21	6.65
Minnesota	1972	371	215	.580	2,651	18	13	7.14
Pro Totals 12-years		4,168	2,290	.549	31,135	234	181	7.47